Haunted Places
of
Shropshire

Rupert Matthews

COUNTRYSIDE BOOKS
NEWBURY, BERKSHIRE

First Published 2005
© Rupert Matthews, 2005

COUNTRYSIDE BOOKS
3 Catherine Road
Newbury, Berkshire

To view our complete range of books,
please visit us at
www.countrysidebooks.co.uk

ISBN 1 85306 938 8
EAN 978 1 85306 938 3

Cover picture from an original
by Anthony Wallis

Photographs by the author

Designed by Peter Davies, Nautilus Design
Typeset by Mac Style Ltd, Scarborough, N. Yorkshire
Produced through MRM Associates Ltd., Reading
Printed by Arrowsmith, Bristol

•Contents•

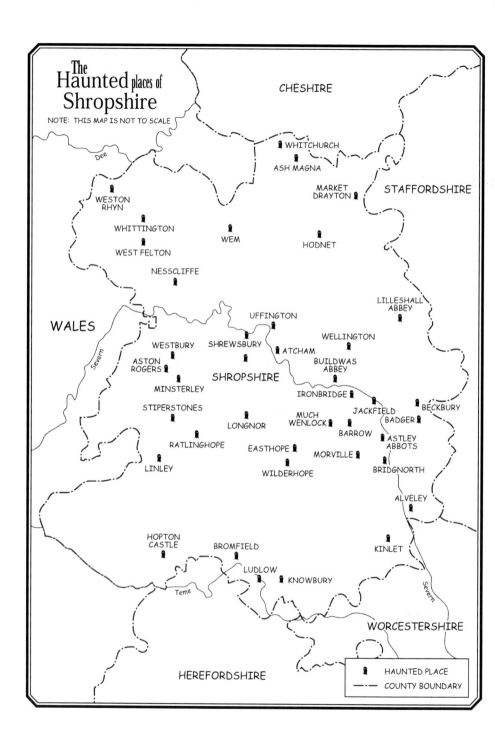

•Introduction•

As one of the most historic counties in England, it is perhaps not surprising that Shropshire is also one of the most haunted. It seems that almost everywhere the traveller turns there is a ghost to be found.

In village streets, town centres and open fields the phantoms crowd round, each with a story behind them and each one unique and dramatic in their way. There are wild warriors mounted on spirited stallions that tear across the landscape with drawn swords and terrifying battle cries. There are gentle maids who flit by as if at complete peace with the world. And there are some truly enigmatic spectres about which little is known except their ability to appear with startling suddenness – only to vanish just as abruptly.

There are some folk who may claim that there are no such things as ghosts. Well, they are entitled to their opinion, of course. But to travel Shropshire and visit the haunted places of this lovely county is to come into close contact with something quite mysterious. When I began these investigations I knew little about the supernatural side of the county. By the time I had spoken to dozens of people about their encounters with the phantoms and spectres of Shropshire, I had no doubt at all that this must rank among the most haunted places on earth.

And there was nothing incredible or fantastic about these ghosts. Unlike the monstrous phantoms to be found in horror movies or books, the ghosts of Shropshire are as much part of the county as the towns, villages and people. They don't leap out to deal death or destruction to all in their path. Indeed, they seem a singularly inoffensive lot – though you never know. They simply appear, go about their own business and then fade back to wherever it is that they came from.

Nor do they appear only in ivy-clad ruins or moonlit graveyards. The pubs and hotels that I visited to track down spooks and spectres have been among the most welcoming and convivial places it has been my pleasure to visit. And when I have been taken to romantically ruined castles, as at Whittington, they have been charming rather than alarming. Indeed that castle is now home to a village trust of apparent efficiency and friendliness.

I must thank the good folk of Shropshire for their help in preparing this volume and for the magnificent welcome that they gave me on my travels. Calling on strangers to ask them about a ghost is not always the best introduction, but the Salopians who I met were unfailingly kind and helpful.

This is a beautiful county with much to see and enjoy. Its highways and byways are a joy to travel and its towns and villages wonderful to visit. If you take my advice, you should get out on the road and find your way around the haunted places of Shropshire. Enjoy yourself, and watch out for the ghosts.

Rupert Matthews

•North Shropshire•

WESTON RHYN

The lanes to the west of the village are the haunt of a phantom coach and a white lady. It is generally said that the lady sometimes rides in the coach, and at other times walks on foot, so it would seem that these two apparently distinct phantoms are, in fact, the same haunting.

The barbaric events that led to the haunting took place in the 1640s when civil war between the supporters of king and parliament stalked across England and Wales. The good folk of Weston Rhyn were supporters of the king, so they refused to pay their taxes to the authorities in Shrewsbury, who backed Parliament. Such action was bound to bring retribution, which duly arrived in the shape of a troop of Roundhead cavalry which came trotting into Weston Rhyn early one morning as the civil war drew to a close.

The troops arrested Miss Phillips, the owner of nearby Tyn-y-Rhos Hall, and rounded up the villagers. Even at swordpoint the villagers refused to hand over their cash. The troopers built up a huge fire, placing on it a large cauldron of water. As this water grew scalding hot, they lowered into it Miss Phillips, then pulled her out and threw her into the chilly waters of the nearby stream. It was too much. The villagers not only paid their taxes, but also handed over a Catholic priest who had been hiding nearby.

The jubilant soldiers bound the priest and Miss Phillips, hauling them off to Chirk for prompt execution. It was soon after this that the quiet phantom of Miss Phillips began to be seen walking the lanes around her old home. The ghostly coach is seen less frequently, but is a rather more spectacular apparition as it trots by pulled by four grey horses.

The second ghostly apparition at Weston Rhyn is unconnected with that of Miss Phillips. This is the ghost of a young man who served in France

The lane at Weston Rhyn along which the phantom coach has been seen approaching the village.

during the Great War. The unfortunate soldier suffered badly in one of the first gas attacks, before the British had learned how to cope with this new German weapon. His lungs were terribly burned and he was no longer fit for active service. He was sent home to the clear air of Shropshire, but never fully recovered and died a few months later. His sad phantom is not seen often, but exudes an air of melancholy when it is encountered.

WHITTINGTON

The village of Whittington stands astride what is now the B5009, but was for many centuries the main road from London to north Wales and Holyhead, from where ferries plied to Ireland. The rich agricultural lands around the River Perry made this a prosperous place as well as one with strategic transport links.

It was, therefore, with some delight that a Norman knight by the name of Fulk Fitzwarin gained the castle and estates of Whittington from his father-in-law, the powerful baron Jocas de Dinan. The fortress and lands came as part of the dowry for Fulk's new bride Hawise de Dinan. In 1198 Fulk died, leaving his lands to his son, the third member of the Fitzwarin family to bear the name of Fulk. This Fulk III was a colourful character, but he at once had a problem. The Dinan family declared that Whittington had been granted to Fulk II for his lifetime only and could not be inherited by Fulk III.

For two years, young Fulk pursued his claim to Whittington through the courts. But in the year 1200 he got bored with the delays and procrastinations imposed by King John. Fulk picked up his sword, rode to Whittington with a band of supporters and grabbed the castle by force. At the time King John was busy on the Continent fighting against King Philip of France and various rebels. Even so, it is unlikely that rash young Sir Fulk could have held the castle against royal troops. But the Dinan family had sided with the King of France, so John was quite happy to deprive them of a key fortress on the Welsh Marches. In 1204, Whittington was officially given to Fulk, on condition that he modernise the defences and hold the castle against any Welsh raids into England.

Sir Fulk was, naturally, delighted. He set about rebuilding the castle with gusto. Until then, Whittington had been a timber fortress with extensive earthworks and a central stone tower. Despite much later alteration, it is the fortifications of Sir Fulk III that make up the ruins of Whittington Castle today. The mighty twin towers that face out across the moat to the main road were the gatehouse of the outer bailey. These buildings served as a village court and a farmhouse for many years, so they have survived in better condition than the much stouter and stronger defences of the inner bailey to the south.

The rebuilding of the castle was completed in around 1233. Sir Fulk fought the Welsh several times, holding his lands and castle stoutly for the King of England. He died in around 1255 at the age of 80. Given the trouble he went to in order to secure Whittington, and the money and care he lavished on the castle, there can be little surprise that the phantom of

Sir Fulk III Fitzwarin returns so often to his old home. Clad in armour of the early 13th century, Sir Fulk has been seen riding about Whittington and nearby lands, usually on wild tempestuous days when winds blow in from Wales and rain clouds scud the sky. It seems his ghost is as tempestuous as was Sir Fulk himself.

Within twenty years of his death, Sir Fulk had become the subject of a lengthy medieval epic poem, of which only parts have been preserved. He is said to have undertaken fantastic adventures in his home territories and further afield.

He is not, however, linked directly to the other ghosts of Whittington. These are the pale-faced phantoms of two children who stare out of the windows of the surviving gatehouse. They are never seen from inside the structure, only by passers-by glancing up at the grim walls. It is not entirely clear who these two youngsters might be, but it is said that they are linked to the great Glyndwr rebellion of the early 1400s. Owain Glyndwr was leading an uprising of the Welsh against the imposition of English law and

The gatehouse of Whittington Castle from which a pair of plaintive ghosts are seen peering.

The corner tower of the inner stronghold at Whittington from which the phantom knight has been seen riding.

English taxes in Wales by King Henry IV. The children may have been hostages taken by Sir Fulk X Fitzwarin for the good behaviour of nearby Welshmen. If so, their fate is unknown. Only the sad faces of their ghosts stare out from their prison.

The castle of Whittington remained in the Fitzwarin family until the death of Fulk XI in 1420, when it passed to his sister who married into the Hankeford family. It is still owned by her descendants, though the care of the castle is in the hands of a Trust dedicated to its repair and maintenance.

WEST FELTON

The village of West Felton is divided by the modern A5, which carries its load of thundering traffic through a cutting that bisects the village. The old main road, now a quiet side road, runs beside the village pub and forms its high street, though the church stands on the other side of the modern road.

The ghost here is that of a former vicar, the Revd Pritchard. He so loved the village that he built a magnificent new home on the outskirts. The beautiful house is known today as Pradoe and stands in extensive wooded grounds half a mile to the south-east of the village centre. Dressed in a black coat, as befits his calling in life, the Revd Pritchard has been seen several times walking between the ancient church and his new home. Perhaps he is keen to return to the two buildings he loved so much when alive.

NESSCLIFFE

The modern A5 swoops past Nesscliffe, carrying juggernauts and cars by the thousand on their way to and from north Wales. Before the modern dual carriageway was constructed, however, the road ran through the village of Nesscliffe on its way from Shrewsbury to Oswestry.

Just before the old road enters the village it runs beneath a towering hill with, on the left, the Three Pigeons pub and a small war memorial on the

The stretch of the old Holyhead Road outside the Three Pigeons at Nesscliffe. It was here that a notorious highwayman had his lair, and where his ghost returns to recreate his lawless ways.

right. Today, this is a welcoming place where the pub offers good food and fine ales to travellers and locals alike. But in Tudor times this was a dangerous and forbidding place. So risky was passing this way, that the wool merchants' guild in Shrewsbury hired tough mercenary ex-soldiers to escort its members to Oswestry on their way to buy wool from Welsh sheep farmers.

The main problem came in the form of a daring and violent highway robber by the name of Sir Humphrey Kynaston. This Sir Humphrey had been born into wealth and privilege, but as soon as he inherited his lands around Myddle, he drank and gambled his inheritance away. Scorning anything so common as working for a living, Kynaston became a robber, finding easy prey among the travellers on the road to Oswestry. He lived in a cave set high up on the hill above Nesscliffe, where he carved himself a fine chair out of the living rock.

It was the feats of Kynaston's horse that gave rise to the rumours that he was in league with the Devil. Pursued by his enemies, Kynaston once jumped his horse over the River Severn itself, a distance of 40 feet. On another occasion he was trapped inside a yard at Aston, but his horse leapt the 12-foot-tall gates to freedom.

It is no wonder that the towering figure of a huge man mounted on a gigantic black horse that has been seen galloping past the Three Pigeons is said to be Sir Humphrey Kynaston. Whether this is, indeed, the legendary outlaw returning to his old haunts on his satanic steed or some quite different phantom is hard to judge. Perhaps it is best to believe the old stories, they are certainly the romantic option.

WEM

Back in 1677 the old town hall at Wem was burnt down. The fire was begun accidentally by a young girl named Jane Churm, who died in the conflagration that followed. It was a tragedy that led to a persistent haunting.

The new town hall that rose up on the scorched site was quickly realised to be haunted. Those who worked there became accustomed to seeing the lively figure of young Jane Churm skipping about the place, running up stairs, darting in and out of rooms. She became a part of the building. If the ghost was seen rather less often as the years passed, she never quite vanished for good.

And then on 19 November 1995 the new town hall, by then over three centuries old, went up in flames. Those who gathered to watch the fire were certain that they saw the figure of Jane Churm standing on the stairs as they vanished in the smoke. One local man took a photo, which clearly showed the girl standing apparently indifferent to the destruction wrought around her. She has not been seen on the site since. Perhaps two fires were enough.

Just west of Wem lie Loppington Woods. Like the old town hall, these seem to be free of supernatural activity these days, but in the late 19th century they gained international fame for what was seen to go on there. It seems that a poltergeist took up residence. For several months houses there were plagued by broken crockery, flying cups, loud thumps and knocking noises. At Christmas 1883 the disturbances faded, never to return.

HODNET

The Bear Hotel in this old town, dominated by black and white timber architecture, takes its name from the fact that for many years it was home to a bear pit. It was here that the local folk engaged in the ancient pastime of bear baiting. A brown bear was secured by a chain to a stake in the centre of the pit, then hunting dogs were let loose into the pit. Bets were taken on how long the bear would last and how many dogs it might kill before it died.

Thankfully, the pub these days offers less bloodthirsty entertainments and fine foods. Back in the 1680s a Welsh gentleman by the name of Jasper would stop here when travelling to Shrewsbury on business. Whether it was the

The Bear Hotel in Hodnet plays host to a phantom who died a tragic death nearby.

hearty meals or the bear baiting that first attracted him, we do not know, but he enjoyed the inn's hospitality so much that he became a regular guest. He was popular too, paying in good gold coin and standing drinks for the locals.

Then he came one time with neither gold nor silver. He explained that he had lost his fortune speculating in stocks and shares in London. Wearing only a thin coat in the bitterest of winter weather, he asked the landlord for a night's lodging and some hot food to see him through. He promised to pay when he had regained his wealth. The landlord, clearly a hard-hearted man, refused. It was ready cash or nothing. Despite the many times Jasper had stayed and paid well, the landlord turned him out into the snow.

A few hours later the landlord left the bar to fetch something from the store cupboard. He screamed aloud and staggered backwards into the bar, pointing in horror towards the cupboard. Desperately struggling for breath the landlord tried to say something, then pitched forward stone dead. The customers gingerly investigated the cupboard, but it was empty of anything except the stored provisions to be expected. A doctor was summoned who declared the landlord had died of a terrific shock or fright.

Next morning as the folk of Hodnet began gathering for a mid-winter funeral, they found a second body. This was the corpse of Jasper that lay under a hedge where he had clearly sought shelter from the bitter weather, only to freeze to death. On his face was a broad smile of clear joy and happiness. Had he somehow returned to the inn in spectral form to cause the death of the mean-spirited landlord? That at least was the story that ran around Hodnet that chill winter's day as a double funeral took place.

These days, there can be little doubt that Jasper is seen in ghostly form. He appears most often, not in the bar or store room, but in the upstairs corridor. Dressed as in his glory days, he wears a richly embroidered velvet coat as he walks

Jasper, the ghost of the Bear Hotel at Hodnet, was a wealthy Welsh gentleman in life.

slowly from a room towards the stairs. If he harbours any ill will towards the Bear, it is not evident. In fact one person who saw him in the 1990s said that he appeared a jolly and merry soul.

As well he might, for the Bear offers hospitality welcoming enough to make anyone happy.

MARKET DRAYTON

Old Colehurst Manor lies a short distance south of the town of Market Drayton, which still holds its fine Wednesday market, established on the orders of King Edward I. It is tucked away down a narrow lane off a road which itself lies off the A53. It is as well the house is signposted from the main road or visitors may have trouble finding it.

There are a number of ghosts here, but only two appear with any regularity. The most active is seen so often that he is known affectionately as 'Fred', though nobody knows his real name. He is dressed in fashions of the 17th century and has long flowing brown hair and a round, chubby face. It is generally agreed that he is a happy ghost, much given to laughing as if somebody has just told him a joke. When the house was undergoing restoration in the 1980s, Fred was at his most active. He seemed to take particular interest in the building works, being seen near to where the workmen were busily restoring the former glories of Old Colehurst Manor. It is thought he approved.

The other apparition seen with some frequency is that of three ghosts that sit near one of the downstairs windows. They are of a young couple

Old Colehurst Manor, near Market Drayton, is one of the more haunted houses in Shropshire.

17

who are comforting a toddler. The child is crying, though without any great urgency. Perhaps it has fallen or received a little bump or scrape. Whatever the cause of the distress, it is soon put right by the loving parents. The child ceases its sniffles and the ghosts promptly vanish.

ASH MAGNA

The ghost of Ash Magna manifests itself on the side road leading from the village centre to the church to the north. The descriptions of the ghost are clear and consistent, but throw up as many questions as they answer.

The apparition is that of a tall man dressed in a long black coat that has a hood, or the ghost has a scarf around its neck. The bottom of the coat has not been clearly seen, and one witness thought the ghost floated above the ground without any visible legs. The figure usually has its head turned slightly away, so that its face is not seen.

Perhaps inevitably, the ghost is usually said to be that of a monk in a cloak and cowl. There is no evidence to support this and no monastery is known to have stood hereabouts. Perhaps it is a phantom vicar on his way to the church. Or perhaps it is the ghost of a man who simply liked wearing a long black coat.

Ash Magna's ghost resembles a monk, but may not be what he seems.

WHITCHURCH

The town of Whitchurch takes its name from the imposing white church that once dominated the heart of the town. It was built in the early 9th century by Queen Ethelfleda, daughter of King Alfred the Great, when the area was won back by the English from Viking rule. Ethelfleda dedicated the church to the little-known early English holy man, St Alkmund.

The church she built was enlarged, restored and reworked several times until 31 July 1711 when the entire structure crashed to the ground seconds after the congregation left after evensong. The current church was built to replace it, a painting of the old church being put up in the vestry.

The ghosts of Whitchurch lurk in Blaney's Lane and date to violent, turbulent times. In the 1260s the people of England had become thoroughly exasperated by the corrupt, inefficient and unjust rule of King Henry III. The discontented nobles, merchants and peasants found a leader in Simon de Montfort, Earl of Leicester, and Gilbert de Clare, Earl of Gloucester. In 1264 the king's army was defeated at the Battle of Lewes.

Montfort and Gloucester took control of the government. They sacked the corrupt officials, reformed the tax system and then called a Parliament, which included for the first time ordinary citizens elected by towns and counties as well as churchmen and nobles. The meeting on 20 January 1265 was a great success. The Members of Parliament elected from Shropshire came home to report that all was well with the kingdom. Sadly, it wasn't.

Montfort had two greedy, dishonest sons. They set themselves to diverting royal government revenues into their own pockets. Montfort refused to listen to Gloucester when he brought up the issue. Meanwhile, Prince Edward, the future King Edward I, approached Gloucester. He told Gloucester that he agreed that his father's corrupt rule had to end and that he, Edward, was willing to take over as a legitimate ruler in place of the increasingly arbitrary rule of de Montfort. Parliament, Edward promised, would continue to be consulted and high standards imposed on government officials. After one more argument with de Montfort, Gloucester allied himself to Edward.

The people of Shropshire had a problem. Both sides now promised much the same thing. Should they support Montfort or Gloucester and Edward? In June a small force of Edward's men arrived at Whitchurch demanding loyalty from the town. While the town council met to decide, the soldiers got drunk. They started taking without paying and abused some respectable women. A scuffle broke out, then a fight. The soldiers were ambushed and killed in Blaney's Lane.

The town declared for de Montfort, but the issue was settled a few weeks later at the Battle of Evesham where Simon de Montfort was killed. True to

The ghosts of Whitchurch wear the armour of 13th-century men at arms.

his word, Prince Edward continued with the reforms and with Parliament. The people of Whitchurch may have feared they would be treated as rebels, but not so. Edward imposed a fine for form's sake, but it was a light one. The townsfolk had been forgiven by the future king.

But they had not been forgiven by the restless souls of the men they had killed. The ghosts began to walk. They clanked about in their armour disturbing the rest of the citizens of the town that had brought about their deaths. Those ghosts are still to be met in Blaney's Lane from time to time. They appear alone, in pairs or as a group dressed in the armour of their time. These days they appear sad and quiet rather than the angry, vengeful spirits that past accounts describe. Perhaps time has mellowed them and cooled their anger.

•Central Shropshire•

ASTON ROGERS

The village of Aston Rogers is strung out along a narrow lane off the B4386 as it runs west towards Wales. The houses that straggle alongside either side of the lane merge into the hamlet of Aston Pigot to the south.

It is here that a playful little girl ghost has been seen a few times. The girl wears a blue dress and white mop cap and seems to be quite friendly and playful, though she will duck out of sight if approached. Her clothes would date her to the 1870s or thereabouts, while her age seems to be about 8 years old. Some think she may be a local girl who died in an accident many years ago, but there do not seem to be any firm records of any such fatality.

The cheerful little girl's identity must remain a mystery.

The lane through Aston Rogers is home to a playful phantom.

WESTBURY

ontgomery Road in Westbury is haunted by the spectre of a poor girl who learned, too late, that it can be unwise to string a man along with promises that have no real worth.

In 1895 the Red Lion pub employed a barmaid by the name of Annie, a girl from a neighbouring village who lived in as a domestic servant. Soon after she arrived, Annie attracted the attentions of Mr Wigley, the local butcher. This Mr Wigley was not a bad-looking chap and whenever he arrived he always brought a little gift of flowers, prime meat or other trifles. Young Annie enjoyed the attention and encouraged Mr Wigley to assume that she felt romantic attachments to him that did not, in fact, exist.

The sign of the Red Lion in Westbury marks the site of a brutal murder and a dramatic haunting.

After some weeks, Annie found a young man who did take her fancy and decided it was time to end the visits from Mr Wigley. The distraught butcher had believed, and most people thought with good reason, that Annie had returned his feelings. He was appalled to learn that she had merely been playing him along to gain his little presents, but without a thought for his feelings. He stormed out of the Red Lion.

Minutes later Mr Wigley was back, armed with a razor sharp meat cleaver. He sliced down at Annie, catching her a glancing blow on the arm. As she turned to flee she left a bloody handprint on the bar, and a second on the wall of the corridor leading to the back door that gave out on to

Montgomery Road. Opening the door took Annie crucial seconds, and Wigley caught up with her just outside. A single hack with the cleaver was enough to split open the girl's skull and end her life.

Wigley was overpowered by villagers and sent to Shrewsbury for trial. There could be no doubt of his guilt and barely a month later his body was swinging from the hangman's noose in Shrewsbury prison.

Soon afterwards the ghost of Annie began to be seen outside the pub. She seemed to be standing and staring as if lost or bewildered. Perhaps the sudden death that overtook her was such a shock that her poor spirit was unable to understand what was happening.

In the 1970s the old Red Lion was pulled down and a modern pub put up in its place. The change seems to have had an effect on Annie's ghost. She still appears from time to time, but in a less solid form than before. One man compared the ghost to a dense patch of smoke that turned in on itself, but stayed stationary despite the brisk wind blowing at the time.

Perhaps she is finally finding some peace.

MINSTERLEY

The wild country around Minsterley is, even today, remote. Narrow lanes with grass growing through the tarmac wind through the dense forests and up the steep hillsides. In centuries gone by this was almost an inaccessible wilderness, so it made an ideal hideout for the local known to history as Edric the Wild.

Edric Salvage, to give him his correct name, was born at Weston under Redcastle in about 1035 and held estates in southern Shropshire. Ill health stopped Edric from joining his king, Harold Godwinson, at the Battle of Hastings in 1066 so he was alive and well when the new Norman rulers of England came to take possession of Shropshire. At first all was well. But then the Normans began to ignore age-old English laws and English customs. Men were flogged and hanged for breaking Norman laws. They turned to Edric, the sole remaining English lord in possession of his estates in the area.

The fields and hills around Minsterley are the haunt of the legendary Wild Edric.

Edric travelled to the court of King William the Norman to protest against the unjust new laws, but was cuffed aside and treated rudely. Coming home, Edric picked up his sword and raised rebellion. He captured Hereford, but failed to storm Shrewsbury. King William came down with the royal army to restore order, forcing Edric to flee to the wild lands around the Long Mynd. Here Edric married an elfin bride, gaining the help and protection of the little people who abounded in these forests in those days.

The Normans never captured Edric the Wild, who continued to pursue his own war against the invaders for years. Eventually Edric's attacks became less frequent, then halted altogether. The Normans hoped Edric was dead, but the English whispered that he merely slept among the wild hills, ready to return should the English need him.

To this day walkers on the hills will report seeing a tall man dressed in green and mounted on a great white stallion. This is Wild Edric, riding out over the hills to see if he is needed. He was seen, leading his band of armed men, just before the Crimean War and appeared again with his men when

24

In 1067 Edric the Wild mustered the men of Minsterley and the surrounding area for war.

Hitler's hordes camped in northern France awaiting a chance to invade England. Since then he seems to have appeared alone, presumably because no foreign invader threatens the English – yet.

LONGNOR

The White Lady of Longnor is one of the most famous ghosts in Shropshire. Pick up almost any anthology of ghost stories and the beautiful phantom of Longnor will more than likely be included. The details of the story vary from account to account, but the outline remains the same.

Some 200 years ago or so, no firm date can be found, a pretty teenage girl of Longnor fell deeply in love with a well-heeled farmer from Church

Stretton, or Much Wenlock, or perhaps from Shrewsbury. Wherever he was from, the wealthy gentleman paid court assiduously to the young girl from Longnor and in due course proposed. The delighted girl accepted, and arrangements were made for the wedding.

Come the wedding day the bride arrived at the church of Longnor with her proud family and friends to find no sign of the prospective groom. A few minutes later a boy arrived on a pony carrying an envelope addressed to the girl. It was a curt, heartless note from the man breaking off the engagement. Overcome with grief, the girl ran from the church, raced down to the bridge over the stream that runs just west of the village and threw herself into the swirling waters. Her body was found some miles downstream next day.

The ghost is to be seen on or near the fatal bridge, now replaced by a modern road bridge. She is dressed in her long, white wedding dress and stands staring forlornly at the waters as they flow away beneath her feet. Some accounts claim that she will drift eerily through the parapet of the bridge to fall slowly into the stream and fade gently from view. Others maintain that she simply vanishes from sight while standing on the bridge. All agree that the girl is young and slim, with a strikingly pretty face for those who see her that closely.

More dramatic accounts have it that the ghostly White Lady of Longnor does not confine herself to drifting spookily over the bridge. She has been reported attending dances and teenage parties held in the village. There is more than one story of a local young man fancying his chances with the pretty stranger at the party, only to be shocked when she reveals herself to be the ghost by vanishing abruptly or turning to a hideous grinning skull before his eyes. One story even has the young man the worse for drink and trying to grapple with the attractive girl before he realises his awful mistake. Such sensational accounts are, perhaps, best treated with some suspicion for they seem more akin to horror films than to the way real ghosts behave.

That is not to say that there is not a White Lady of Longnor. There are simply too many accounts of a ghostly figure near the bridge for her to be

The White Lady of Longnor is seen most often hovering around the bridge near the village.

ignored. It is clear, however, that the stories have got somewhat out of hand and today include macabre and horrific inventions that are far removed from the tragic tale of a wronged girl who was driven to take her own life by a heartless brute.

SHREWSBURY

S hropshire's ancient county town of Shrewsbury is one of the best-preserved medieval towns in England. The castle still guards the river crossings, while many old buildings crowd in along the medieval street plan.

The town got its start in the 5th century when the inhabitants of the old Roman city at Wroxeter decided they needed to live on a more easily-defended site given the growing anarchy and incessant wars of the Dark Ages. They chose a hill in a loop of the Severn and moved in under the leadership of an ealdorman named Scrobbes, whose name survives in corrupted form in the name of both town and county. The town never looked back.

Although the town's military history has been dominated by wars against the Welsh, it was an English civil war that led to the Battle of Shrewsbury in 1403. The battle was fought between King Henry IV and rebellious nobles just north of the town. Strangely the phantom soldiers of Shrewsbury are linked not to this battle, but to the Battle of Bosworth fought in Leicestershire in 1485.

The throne was then held by King Richard III, a competent and efficient ruler with the unfortunate gift of alienating almost everyone who met him. The pretender was Henry Tudor, a young Welsh nobleman with an obscure link to the English royal family and some powerful supporters. Henry landed in Wales with a small mercenary force, gathered men and arms from his Welsh supporters and marched into England. His first night on English soil was spent at Shrewsbury, with his men camped beyond the Severn and a bodyguard lodged just off Wyle Cop in houses flanking what is now known as Barrack's Passage.

On 22 August the Battle of Bosworth was fought to a bloody finish. At the climax of the fighting King Richard spurred his horse towards Henry Tudor, backed by his staunchest supporters. Richard hacked his way towards the rebel, cutting down

The old houses of Shrewsbury's Barrack's Passage once housed medieval soldiers who return here in spectral form.

the bodyguards who had been lodged in Shrewsbury's Barrack's Passage, but was himself killed barely ten yards from his enemy.

Soon afterwards the good people of Shrewsbury began to see and hear the carousing soldiers of Henry Tudor's bodyguard in Barrack's Passage again. Presumably they enjoyed their time in Shrewsbury and return to continue the stay for as long as possible.

Another phantom with military connections lurks in the Dun Cow pub, a little distance over the Severn to the east. This pub was built in 1085 to house the master masons in charge of construction work then going on at the new Abbey of St Peter and St Paul, just over the road. The building later served as lodgings for visitors to the Abbey before being converted into an inn at the Reformation. In the 1590s it was extended to suit its new role. The timbers for the extension came from a Spanish ship, captured during the fighting that

The Dun Cow pub stood just outside the town walls and was chosen by Prince Rupert as the royalist headquarters for Shropshire in the Civil War.

The main bar at the Dun Cow. It was here that the resident ghost put in an appearance in the autumn of 2004.

Shrewsbury's Prince Rupert Hotel has a mischievous spirit lurking within its walls.

defeated the Spanish Armada in 1588, which was then being broken up at Bristol.

In 1644 the building served as the headquarters for Prince Rupert when he commanded the troops of his uncle, King Charles I, during the English Civil War. Late one evening a Dutch officer acting as military adviser to the young prince got involved in a quarrel with a town steward called Sir Richard. In the brawl that followed, Sir Richard was killed. Next morning the Dutchman was hauled in front of Prince Rupert. Ever a stickler for proper behaviour by soldiers to civilians, Prince Rupert sentenced the killer to death and let it be known that any soldier who was tempted to misuse the citizens of Shrewsbury would get similarly severe treatment.

The Dutchman was reportedly indignant and right to the end refused to believe his skills would be dispensed with in such brutal fashion. 'But I only killed one Englishman,' he protested on his way to execution. He was hanged from a hastily improvised gibbet outside the Dun Cow.

His ghost is still annoyed by what happened, or so it would seem. Dressed in the uniform of a cavalry officer with jingling spurs and clanging sword, he has been seen striding about the pub and the old stables ever since. His most recent appearance was in September 2004 when he was seen walking through the bar towards the rear of the building.

The restaurant of the Prince Rupert Hotel has had its share of pranks by the supernatural trickster.

In Butcher Row, at the heart of the old town, stands the Prince Rupert Hotel. This is another ancient inn, dating back to around 1180. The ghost here is an enigmatic entity, if it is a single ghost that is.

The more disturbing of the various phantoms is that of a young woman who committed suicide in one of the upstairs rooms by hanging herself from a wooden beam. The ghost of this poor girl has been seen dangling by the thin rope that ended her life in the room where she died. In 2004 one American guest staying in the room returned from a day's sightseeing. Moments later he came racing down to reception to report a dead body in his room. Not until the manager had personally visited the room and explained did he calm down.

The corridors of the upper floors are said to be haunted by an elderly man who potters about holding a candle as if searching for his room, or perhaps a bathroom. Given that he wears a long nightshirt, it is impossible to date this ghost with any real accuracy, but it is generally thought that he is an owner of the hotel from Victorian days.

The manager of the hotel in 2005 formed his own conclusions after nine years of looking after this elegant and luxurious hotel. 'I feel there is a mischievous personality within the hotel,' he claims. Certainly a spiritual practical joker might account for the variety and frequency of the manifestations that take place there.

Between the Prince Rupert Hotel and the town gates stands the Lion Hotel in Wyle Cop. An inn of this name has stood on the site since the 14th century, and it is believed that the young Prince Hal, later King Henry V, stayed here the night after winning the Battle of Shrewsbury in 1403.

The fine statue of a lion that has welcomed visitors to the Lion Hotel in Shrewsbury for over 150 years.

The cellars at the Lion Hotel. In October 2004 the ghost materialised in this doorway, then moved away to the right.

Certainly a hotel of this name was here in 1618. It is thought, however, that the current building dates back only to around 1630, though the cellars may belong to the earlier building.

However old the cellars may be, they are certainly home to the first of the ghosts to lurk in this fine hotel. This ghost may be ancient for he does not seem to be able to manifest himself properly. A barman who went down to the cellars in October 2004 had a typical sighting. He reported catching a glimpse of a slight movement to his left. Turning round to see who had followed him to the storeroom, he saw a white shape gradually forming out of thin air. As the man watched, the shape coalesced into a human outline, though it was impossible to discern any clear features. The gradually thickening shape seemed to be made of dense white mist or smoke that was pulling itself together. The figure then moved across the room from the doorway towards the far wall. As it approached the wall the shape seemed to give up trying to manifest itself and dissipated as silently as it had first appeared.

Unsurprisingly this particular man has since refused to go down the cellar alone and will always persuade someone else to accompany him when he needs to descend the steps to the dark subterranean chamber.

Almost as insubstantial is the phantom military man who occupies a comfortable seat in the main lounge on the ground floor. Appearing to date from the height of the British Empire, this splendidly robust figure sits four-square with bristling military whiskers and a bright red army tunic. This imposing, yet somehow genial chap is not seen often, and then not for more than a second or two.

The most often-seen phantom at the Lion, however, is the well-known Old Lady. So frequently seen is this ghost, and in such detail, that a portrait of her has been painted that hangs over the fireplace in the lounge.

She seems to be particularly attracted to the grand ballroom on the first floor. This sumptuous room was built following designs by the noted interior designer Robert Adam in 1770. The then owner of the hotel, Richard Lawrence, ran his own coach service to London and on to Holyhead and was one of the richest and most respected men in Shrewsbury. He established the Lion as the centre for the social life of the town; a reputation that long survived his death. In 1830 the original Madam Tussaud brought her waxworks here, followed the next year by the famous Italian violin virtuoso Niccolo Paganini who put on two concerts in the ballroom, and in 1849 by the singer Jenny Lind, 'The Swedish Nightingale', who sang here again in 1856.

We do not know if the ghostly Old Lady attended any of these shows, or if she was present for one of the glittering balls that drew the very cream of society from Shropshire and surrounding counties. Given her behaviour, it does seem likely. She is seen often at one end of the ballroom, close to the stairs. It is as if she is waiting for somebody, glancing

This portrait depicts the ghost seen most often at the Lion and hangs in the downstairs lounge of the hotel.

34

The elegant ballroom of the Lion Hotel. The lady ghost first appears here, then walks downstairs to the side door of the hotel.

occasionally along the room as if seeking a face in a crowd. Finding whatever, or whoever, she has been seeking, the Old Lady then turns and walks down the stairs to the entrance hall, now the hotel reception. She walks across the room to leave the hotel by what is now a fire exit, but was the main entrance until a refurbishment in the 20th century.

The Old Lady never takes any notice of mortals who she might encounter on her route. Nor is she much troubled by closed doors, through which she glides as if they are not there. Nor does she vary her routine at all. She may only be seen for part of her route each time, but she always determinedly follows her set path from ballroom to street.

One member of staff, a chambermaid, who encountered the ghost in the summer of 2004 knew at once who she was looking at. The ghostly figure came along the corridor out of the ballroom with calm, unhurried steps and in complete silence. She was perfectly solid and appeared quite real, but her old-fashioned clothes gave her away as did the total silence with which she moved. The Old Lady walked briskly, but was in view for five or six seconds during which time the chambermaid could take in every detail of her dress. As soon as the ghost was gone, the woman hurried downstairs to the portrait in the lounge to compare the figure she had seen with the woman in the painting. The face was not quite right, she thought, but the clothes were absolutely correct.

Rather more sinister is the cursed room at the Nag's Head Inn on the opposite side of Wyle Cop from the Lion. This timbered building dates back to the 17th century and for many years served as a coaching inn for the humbler sort of traveller, while the fashionable gentry made for the Lion further up the hill. The best rooms at the Nag's Head were for the paying customers; the staff and coachmen slept upstairs in the suite of tiny rooms beneath the roof.

In one of these little rooms, usually kept firmly locked these days, is a cupboard on the inside of which is painted a portrait of what looks like an Old Testament prophet. This room, and the painting in particular, have attracted an evil reputation. In the 1850s a coachman staying overnight drank rather more than was good for him and, on retiring to sleep in the room, made fun of the painting. Next day he hanged himself. Some years later a young lady likewise laughed at the serious, sacred expression on the portrait's face. She too died the following day.

It is the coachman's ghost, that is said to lurk in the little room and the corridor outside. Although the tiny room is kept locked, a flickering light as if from a candle will sometimes be seen late at night. More solid is the thick-set phantom man in a long coat who walks out of the room and along the corridor, only to vanish before reaching the stairs.

The castle that stands on the highest point of the hill on which Shrewsbury stands has a most disturbing phantom. This is the ghost of Bloundie Jack, a murderer from the 14th century who was brought to justice here. Throughout the medieval period and beyond, Shrewsbury castle served as the main prison and courthouse for the county, and it was here that executions were usually carried out.

Bloundie Jack was a tall, muscular fellow who lived on one of the farms outside the town walls. He was notorious for preferring his own company to that of others and his house was rather run-down. Otherwise he seemed perfectly normal and certainly worked hard and dealt honestly. Nobody suspected the truth.

Then a teenage girl named Fanny went missing from Shrewsbury. Fanny was a good girl who would never stay out late nor dally with strangers, so her family knew at once that something was wrong. Her elder sister roused the family's neighbours and friends to organise a search. It was quickly found that the missing girl had been seen talking to Bloundie Jack a couple of hours earlier.

The spirited sister at once led a select group of the stronger young men among the gathering crowd out of the town gates and over the Severn to Bloundie Jack's house. At first the farmer refused the group access to his house, declaring he did not bother them in their houses, so why should they bother him in his. The witness who had seen Fanny with Bloundie Jack was adamant she had not been mistaken, so the stout Shrewsbury lads pounced on Bloundie Jack and held him firmly while the sister pushed her way into the house. She found more than she bargained for.

Stretched out dead on the floor was the body of poor Fanny. The motives for her abduction and murder were all too clear by the state of her clothing. But the gruesome and bizarre nature of the discovery was the carving knife lying beside the body and the carefully severed fingers arranged in a neat row. The sister staggered out to get air and reveal what she had found. Bloundie Jack was hauled off to be locked up in the castle while the authorities were sent for.

A careful search of the house revealed even more disturbing evidence. Kept neatly in an upstairs cabinet, carefully tied up in squares of cloth, were the decomposing severed fingers of eight other women. Enquiries revealed the names of several girls who had supposedly left to take up jobs as domestic servants in some distant town, only to be not heard from again. Clearly Bloundie Jack was what we would today call a serial killer. The honest folk of 14th-century Shrewsbury contented themselves with

The main gates of Shrewsbury Castle, through which the ghost has been seen to walk.

calling him an evil ogre and hanging him from the castle walls just days later.

It is the ghost of this ogre that haunts the green turf of the lawns within the castle. Some say the shambling brute of a man plods around the courtyard glaring around him with fear and hate. Other descriptions have him dragging a girl by her hair across the courtyard. But whatever he is seen to be doing, this phantom exudes a most unpleasant aura. One person had to leave the castle grounds at high speed on seeing the ghost, and has not returned there since, despite living only 150 yards away above a shop in the town centre.

Outside Shrewsbury town centre, the Albright Hussey Hotel occupies an ancient manor house that was built in 1524. While Prince Rupert stayed at the Dun Cow, a regiment of his cavalry was quartered here, after which the manor gently slipped into obscurity as a home of the local Piggot family. In 1988 it was bought by the hotelier Franco Subbiani who began a rolling programme of refurbishment to return the house to its full Tudor glory, while incorporating modern luxuries.

The resident ghost would seem to approve, for it is now as active as ever. Mr Subbiani has himself experienced attentions from the ghost when sleeping in one of the bedrooms. Twice he was woken up by the sounds of banging, though he knew full well he was alone in that part of the building.

On another occasion a honeymoon couple were staying in one of the luxury suites in the older part of the building. The bride woke up in the middle of the night and saw a very tall man standing by the end of the bed. He was wearing a black hat, long black coat and had his face wrapped in a scarf. The figure was present only for a moment before fading away to nothingness.

Strangely, the photos taken in that room of the bride just before the wedding show what seems to be a baby sitting on the bed, although no baby was present. Nine months later to the day the bride gave birth to a baby, which strongly resembled the mysterious figure in the photo.

ATCHAM

The elegant and comfortable Mytton and Mermaid Hotel beside the river at Atcham is one of the few hotels in England to be named after its ghost. For this welcoming hotel is the haunt of Sir Jack Mytton, one of the most colourful men ever to have lived in Shropshire.

'Mad Jack', as Mytton was generally known, was born in 1796 at Halston as the sole son and heir of one of the richest and most ancient families among the Shropshire gentry. He could trace his ancestry back to the 11th century with ease and boasted links to the grandest titles in England. As he grew into young adulthood, Jack proved to be not only athletic and handsome, but charming and witty as well. He was a crack shot and a skilled horseman of national fame. He was also decidedly odd. His father had died when he was a child, and his mother was quite unable to control him.

At the age of 21 Mytton came into a fortune of £60,000 cash and £10,000 a year in rent from land. It was a colossal amount of money.

Mytton decided to enjoy the new-found wealth. He began with an extended holiday in Europe that lasted many months and took him to most of the large cities and capitals of the continent. On his return he joined the army, gaining a commission in the 7th Hussars, one of the most fashionable cavalry regiments. But he did not get on with military discipline and resigned. He then bought a stable of racehorses, adding any horse that caught his fancy, and embarked on a career as a trainer, rider and owner of racehorses.

In 1822 he married Caroline Giffard, daughter of Squire Giffard of Chillington. She proved herself to be as high-spirited as her husband. She threw herself into the lifestyle of being married to Mad Jack. She hosted the parties he threw for his tenants, rode to hounds with him and enthusiastically backed his horses at the various race meets they attended. In 1823, Mytton became High Sheriff of Shropshire and was elected Mayor of Oswestry and MP for Shrewsbury.

He got himself a highwayman's outfit and took great delight in holding up men he invited over for dinner, only to return their property later that evening. Tiring of this stunt, he then trained one of his horses to enter the dining room and leap over the table during dinner. A few months later this became too dull, so he bought a trained bear and learned to ride it, taking great delight in surprising his guests with a sudden appearance on bear-back.

His driving was skilful, but hazardous. He once tried to leap a tollgate while driving his carriage, with predictably messy consequences, and another time deliberately turned over his coach on hearing his companion remark that he had never been in a road accident. Meanwhile, his riding skills were as formidable as ever. He loved hunting, keeping his own pack of hounds and riding out nearly every day of the season. One winter's day he found himself miles from home as heavy snow began to fall. He walked into the farmhouse of a tenant, settled his horse down in front of the kitchen range for warmth and promptly fell asleep for the night. Another time he got drenched falling into a ditch only to swap his soggy coat and breeches for a red woollen nightdress owned by a hapless woman living nearby.

During the bitterly cold winter of 1826 he bought all his servants skates so that they could go out on the frozen lake on his estate. Later he went out duck shooting on the ice clad only in his nightgown and caught a severe chill that brought him close to death.

Soon after recovering, Mytton's habitual heavy drinking got out of hand. Unfortunately the popularity and admiration that he had by now gained seems to have gone to his head. What had previously been high-spirited generosity and eccentricity began to get seriously out of hand. He was drinking up to nine bottles of a port a day at one point.

He began to spend more and more time in pubs and inns of dubious character, mixing with rogues and crooks. He got involved in vicious brawls and was caught with prostitutes. His wife left him and his friends abandoned him.

Eventually, Mytton's own mother had him examined by doctors who declared him insane. He was put in the care of three burly keepers and kept firmly locked up. But in 1834 bailiffs employed by men to whom Mytton owed money called and hauled the poor man away. He was put in a debtors' prison to await trial, but died of an infection within days.

When Mytton's body began its final journey from Shrewsbury to Halston for burial, the entire county was united in grief for their eccentric,

The Mytton and Mermaid Hotel at Atcham takes its name from the ghost that lurks here.

The elegant bridge over the Severn at Atcham. It was over this bridge that the most spectacular funeral procession in Shropshire's history came in 1834.

mad but much-loved squire. Church bells tolled as the coffin was loaded on to a hearse, every shop in Shrewsbury was closed and thousands of people lined the route as the cortege crossed the bridge into Atcham. The procession halted at what is now the Mytton and Mermaid, then the Berwick Arms. There the coffin was set to rest on trestles in a room overlooking the river so that locals could come to pay their respects.

Next morning the coffin containing the body of Mad Jack Mytton left to travel to the chapel where the funeral took place. It was one of the grandest and, with 3,000 mourners, most attended funerals ever held in Shropshire.

For some reason Mytton's ghost returns yet to the room where his body rested the night before the funeral. Dressed in a riding coat and high boots, the archetypal mad squire stands quietly gazing out of the window at the

The room where the ghost of Jack Mytton has been seen standing in quiet contemplation.

flowing waters of the Severn as it swirls beneath Atcham Bridge, over which his funeral cortege travelled. Perhaps the wayward squire is quietly contemplating his life, with its wild escapades and sad ending.

The room where he is seen is, today, a drawing room for the luxurious hotel that now occupies the building. It acquired its present name in 1930s when it was completely transformed from a run-down coaching inn to a first-class hotel catering to the newly motorised traveller. The old taproom where Mytton is known to have drunk is now 'Mad Jack's Bar' and holds some memorabilia of the man after whom it is named. The memory of this colourful character is well cared for.

UFFINGTON

The little village of Uffington lies east of Shrewsbury, on a lane between the A5 and A53. The feeling of being rather overlooked by the rushing modern world may come from the fact that its high street is quiet and ignored by the thundering traffic of the two main roads. It is not, however, ignored by the ghosts.

Late in the evening, usually on still summer nights when the warm air hangs heavy, a horseman will gallop up the high street. Heading north at breakneck speed, the rider is an enigmatic figure. He is rarely, if ever, seen. The sound of hooves clattering over the road and the laboured breathing of the horse both indicate that speed is of the utmost importance and that the rider is lashing his mount to ever greater efforts. The sounds begin in the distance coming up from the direction of Upton Magna, reach a crescendo as if the horse and rider are only feet away, then vanish suddenly.

Near the northern end of the high street stands the imposing bulk of the Corbet Arms Hotel. Comfortable and offering a fine selection of ales and meals, the Corbet Arms also gives the visitor the chance to see the phantom of a young girl. She is generally thought to have been lingering as a ghost for 150 years and to have died in some sort of tragic accident in the attic, though details are scarce.

The Corbet Arms at Uffington has a ghostly child inside and a phantom horseman outside.

Just outside Uffington the old Pimley Manor plays host to a female phantom.

The third ghost of Uffington is to be found on the far side of the A49 to the west. Down a narrow lane opposite a modern housing estate is the building that was once Pimley Manor, but is now a complex of offices and industrial units. The ghost to be found here is friendly and exudes an aura of well-being. She takes the form of a young lady dressed in the fashions of the Georgian period, all in a dull-coloured fabric that may be beige or cream.

As with the girl at the Corbet Arms, it is not entirely clear whose ghost this is. She is often said to be a daughter of the house who died of a broken heart after a tragic love affair, but again certainty is impossible. Only the spectral lady herself knows the truth behind her appearances. And she is not telling.

LILLESHALL ABBEY

The phantom monk of Lilleshall Abbey is a most unusual ghost. It is not that phantom monks are particularly rare in Shropshire, it is that this particular spectre has a question and he asks visitors to his abbey about it in the most direct fashion.

The Augustinian abbey was founded in 1148 by a local landowner named Sir Richard de Belmeis. Neither Sir Richard nor the Augustinians spared much expense and within 20 years a magnificent church had been erected in red sandstone, along with some impressive domestic buildings for the monks and their lay staff. The church alone was 228 ft in length and was adorned with much carving and embellishments that were replaced and updated as the years passed.

The abbey was closed down in 1548, but did not at once fall into the ruin it is today. The building and its estates were bought by James Leveson of Wolverhampton, a wealthy merchant desiring a country estate. He converted the church to be a grand house and adapted most of the old monastic buildings to agricultural use. In 1642 the Leveson family declared for the king as the English Civil War got into its stride. Their grand house was used as a supply centre by the king's troops in the Marches, and so attracted the attentions of the Roundhead army, which arrived here in 1645. With their cannon and explosives, the Roundheads made short work of the Cavaliers' hastily erected defences. They then set fire to the Leveson home by way of retribution, which created the ruins we see today.

One of the most famous features of the abbey to have survived both Leveson's rebuilding and the Roundhead fire is the processional doorway at the south-east corner of the nave, leading into the cloister. It was in the cloister than the monks formed up to march through this door into the abbey for divine service six times every day.

It is near here that the black monk is seen most often. He is usually described as being fairly tall and slim, though whether he is middle-aged or elderly seems to be open to debate. Whenever he is seen, the ghost appears to be perfectly real and solid, being neither transparent nor hovering above the ground. Most often he is said to be kneeling or standing with head bowed as if in prayer or deep contemplation. It is then, as if he has suddenly become aware that he is not alone, that the phantom looks up and moves forward. 'Have you found the secret?' he asks. He then stands a moment or two as if trying to remember something, before vanishing into nothingness.

This enigmatic ghost does not always ask his famous question, but sometimes disappears while still knelt in prayer.

There has, of course, been a great deal of speculation as to what the secret of Lilleshall Abbey might be. Some believe that the phantom is guarding a fabulous treasure that was hidden away in 1548 rather than allow it to fall into the hands of the men sent by King Henry VIII to seize the abbey and its assets. Talk of buried gold and jewels may owe more to hope than to reality, but it is known that some abbots hid their monastic treasures in the hope that the Catholic faith would one day return to England.

Others believe that the secret has a far grimmer truth. It is whispered that a brutal murder was carried out here. The finger of suspicion is sometimes pointed at one of England's proudest and most stubborn kings, Henry III. In 1244 the king was desperately short of money. He had spent a fortune on luxurious living and on wars in France, but because he refused to abide by the Magna Carta his nobles and people refused to pay any new taxes. The Magna Carta, signed by Henry's father King John, established or confirmed various freedoms and rights for the people of England. Henry, however, wanted to rule untrammelled by such niceties.

He came to Lilleshall Abbey ostensibly on a hunting trip, but in reality to get his hands on as much money as he could. First he announced that he had secret news that the Welsh were gathering for war and demanded that the men of Shropshire pay an invented tax to provide wages for soldiers to oppose the invasion. But the stout yeomen and nobles of Shropshire were willing to do their own fighting. They turned out armed

The phantom monk of Lilleshall Abbey is thought to be hiding a dark secret.

King Henry III confronts his barons. It was the need for money that brought Henry to Lilleshall Abbey and may have driven him to murder.

to the teeth. The king found himself confronted by an army of tough, armed men, all of whom wanted the Magna Carta obeyed and none of whom had any intention of paying him taxes. Henry announced the Welsh had called off the invasion and sent everyone home again.

Next he tried selling titles and appointments. It was this that led to murder. Among the offices the king put up for sale was the post of county sheriff. In the 13th century the sheriff was a powerful figure. He administered justice, collected taxes and generally supervised all the business of government in his county. Wise kings appointed honest, competent men to be sheriff for the opportunities for corruption were great. Now King Henry was effectively condoning corruption by auctioning the post to the highest bidder.

As might be imagined the then Sheriff of Shropshire was unimpressed. He rode to Lilleshall Abbey to try to persuade the king to change his mind. He rode in, but never rode out. If he was murdered on the orders of the king, perhaps the ghostly black monk knows who did the deed and wishes to bring him to justice. Or perhaps he committed the outrage himself and seeks absolution.

A rather less colourful speculation has it that the ghostly monk is one of the abbots of Lilleshall who condemned a monk to be beaten to death for some crime against the strict rules of the Augustinian Order. Perhaps the monk had indulged in sins of the flesh, or been caught eating meat on a Friday. Whatever his crime it is thought to have been minor. So now the abbot walks the ruins of his monastery filled with remorse for what he has done. If so, he has a good reason to ask if anyone has discovered the secret. He wants to keep it buried for all time.

All that can be said with any real certainty is that the black monk is seen at Lilleshall with some frequency. Whatever has been keeping him tied to this spot over the centuries must be powerful indeed.

WELLINGTON

In the days when the only way to get to Ireland was by ship, the old Roman Watling Street, now the A5, was thronged with merchants and travellers of all sorts on their way to or from the ferry terminal at Holyhead. There was then no such place as the vast sprawling new town at Telford; instead Watling Street ran through small, rural villages such as Oakengates and Wellington.

It was at Wellington that an unfortunate traveller known only as Humphrey decided to stop for the night. As late afternoon turned to dusk, he gave his mare to an ostler to care for and strode into the bar of the Swan Inn. Dressed in a knee-length leather coat flung open to reveal a fancy waistcoat and knee-high riding boots, the man made an arresting figure. Having secured a room for the night, he ordered a meal and drink.

A servant gathered his name was Humphrey, but the inn was busy so conversation was limited and the stranger offered no hint as to his surname nor where he was from.

The servant did notice, however, that he had a bulging pouch of some weight attached to his belt. When the time came to pay, the man in the leather coat opened up the pouch, pulled out a glistening gold sovereign and handed it over as payment, slipping his silver change back into the heavy pouch.

It was later thought that somebody other than the servant must have seen this pouch, and that the temptation proved too much for him. Later that night the landlord was awoken by the sounds of a fight upstairs. Rousing his staff, the man rushed up to find a window thrown open and the body of Humphrey lying dead on the floor. His pouch was missing, and the murderous thief was presumed to have escaped through the window.

The body was respectfully laid out by the good folk of Wellington and given a decent Christian burial. It proved impossible to inform his next of

The Swan Inn at Wellington where a ghost in a leather coat stalks the premises.

The bar in the Swan. It was a careless moment that led to the murder that caused the haunting here.

kin of his fate for nobody knew his name or his home. His grave was marked by a simple wooden cross in case any family members came asking for a missing traveller, but none ever came. Humphrey rests in the churchyard to this day.

But he does not rest easy for his ghost walks the Swan Inn. Wearing his distinctive leather coat he stalks the upstairs corridors and the room where he was murdered. He seems agitated or worried, as well he might considering the fate that overtook him here. Witnesses have said that he moves with quick steps, pacing back and forth. Sometimes it is only the footsteps that are heard, either from a floor below or from one of the rooms, and when they are investigated there is nobody there.

On the opposite side of the road stands the Cock Tavern. This ancient inn was, like the Swan, a thriving and bustling place in the glory days of the coaching trade. Like the Swan it is now a pleasant pub catering mainly to the local populace. And like the Swan it is haunted. This is a more enigmatic phantom, however, to which no real story is attached.

BUILDWAS ABBEY

The year 1342 was not a good time to be a monk at Buildwas Abbey. There was serious trouble afoot, and it was trouble that would lead to murder.

The problems seem to have begun about 18 months earlier when a murrain, or cattle disease, swept through Shropshire. On one manor, not too far from Buildwas, 62 of the 154 cattle died and the rest were described as being too sick to give milk. We don't know the exact effect this blow had on Buildwas for the abbey records were lost at the Reformation, but it was clearly serious enough to cause several monks to question the actions of their abbot, John Burnell.

The Bishop of Coventry, whose predecessor had founded this Cistercian monastery in 1135, had to send a senior cleric to adjudicate in the dispute. Some sort of agreement was reached, but it did not last. The crops did not grow properly the following year across Shropshire, nor did livestock numbers recover properly from the murrain. Many peasants left the land to look for work elsewhere and a fair acreage of less fertile land was abandoned altogether.

At Buildwas it appears that Abbot Burnell refused to take these serious economic problems into consideration. He insisted that the tenant farmers on the abbey lands should pay their rents in full and refused to allow any remission of fees or fines for any excuse whatsoever. The details of what followed have been lost, but the disgruntled tenants and workers found a voice in the person of Thomas Tong, one of the junior monks at Buildwas. A meeting was arranged to discuss matters, and feelings were running high. The meeting turned violent and in the rioting that followed Tong stabbed Abbot Burnell to death.

This time the Bishop of Coventry called on the county sheriff to provide armed men to accompany his representative to Buildwas to sort out the new trouble. Tong was arrested and hauled off for trial. As a monk, Tong was subject to Church justice, not the king's justice, so he escaped hanging for the killing. Instead he was flogged, expelled from the Cistercian Order and commanded to go on pilgrimage to seek forgiveness from God.

A new abbot was appointed to Buildwas and the rent books adjusted to a suitable compromise. The troubles of Buildwas were far from over, sadly. Five years later the Black Death struck the country, killing almost half the population in less than a year. The estates of Buildwas Abbey plummeted in value and produced very little by way of rent. To cap it all Thomas Tong reappeared. He had completed his pilgrimage and, so he said, been forgiven by God. So now he was back wanting to become a monk once again.

The gaunt ruins of Buildwas Abbey show through the trees that flank the Severn.

It all seems to have been too much for the poor spirit of the murdered Abbot Burnell. His ghost was soon seen walking the monastery, apparently unhappy that the rents were not being paid and his killer had returned. Tong made himself scarce, but the phantom found no rest. The lack of money meant that Buildwas never enjoyed a rebuilding in modern style, as did many other religious houses in late medieval times, so it remained the solidly built Norman-style construction that it always had been.

It is these imposing ruins that remain to this day. The monastery was broken up by King Henry VIII in the Reformation and its lands sold off. The Abbot's House and some other buildings were converted into a farm, but the vast bulk of the church was not suitable for conversion to secular use. It was left to fall into decay and ruin, though today decline has been halted by the efforts of English Heritage.

The ghost of Buildwas Abbey wears the white robes of the Cistercian monks who once lived here.

And still the phantom of Abbot Burnell walks his old home. Whether he is angry at the decline of his institution, seeks revenge for his murder or simply finds peace wandering this tranquil and restful site is unknown. Once, in the 1980s, two ghostly monks were seen strolling gently down the roofless nave of the old church. Who Burnell's companion might be is unknown, but perhaps it is some other holy man come to try to find peace for the abbot's restless spirit.

MUCH WENLOCK

The small town of Much Wenlock has not changed much since medieval times. The narrow streets still bustle with local people and many of the older buildings remain. Wenlock gave its name to the dramatic limestone ridge of Wenlock Edge, which runs away to the south-west for miles towards Wales.

The town is still dominated by the great priory that was founded here in the 7th century by the holy English saint, Mildburga. Her foundation was burned down by the Vikings, rebuilt, then torn down and entirely rebuilt by the Normans in 1080 only to be closed down by King Henry VIII during the Reformation that turned England from a Catholic country to a Protestant one.

Strangely, it is not the vast monastery that dominates the supernatural aspect of this pretty town with tales of ghostly monks and spectral abbots, but the more secular side of the town.

The town leapt into the news headlines when a ghost made itself felt in the rather unlikely surroundings of the Spar supermarket, just off The Square. The trouble seems to have begun in 2002 when a refurbishment of the supermarket entailed some substantial building work. New foundations were being dug when a workman came across a human skull. The police were sent for, but it was quickly realised the bones were very old indeed and archaeologists were called in.

A preliminary dig, followed by a more extensive dig in the county archives, revealed that the site had once been the burial ground for the townsfolk. In the 12th century an alehouse was erected on the site, and it had been covered by buildings ever since. Clearly the human remains were of medieval inhabitants of Much Wenlock. The spirits of the long-departed had not seemed to mind being buried under a pub, houses or a supermarket, but they did not appear to take kindly to being dug up and removed to another resting place, no matter how carefully the work was done.

As soon as the refurbishment was finished, the haunting began. At first it took the form of odd happenings that could be put down to faulty memory or simple mistakes. Trolleys were found disorganised when they had been tidied up the evening before. Food tins were in the wrong place on the shelves. Then things took a new turn.

A grey, shadowy figure was seen hovering near the tills by a member of staff stacking shelves after the public had gone. Then the assistant manageress heard what sounded like a person breathing heavily after a long run. This time the invisible visitor was near the door to the staff rooms. The events culminated when the shadowy figure was seen on the same day as a checkout girl felt an invisible hand grasp her firmly on the shoulder.

It was all very unnerving for staff and for shoppers. The haunting was featured on the BBC *Midlands Today* news programme as the haunting reached its most active. In more recent months the haunting seems to have been fading. Presumably whatever was disturbed by the building work has become more settled and is resting more peacefully again.

Another property in Much Wenlock to house an intermittent haunting is

The jocular sign for Much Wenlock's haunted pub gives some indication of the jovial atmosphere within.

Raynald's Mansion in the High Street. Built in 1682, this fine half-timbered building has served many purposes over the years. It is only when it is empty, however, that it is haunted. The faces of two young children are seen peering out of the upper windows by passers-by. Those who do not know the story of the haunting have more than once reported to police that children are trapped in the empty building, but the police have given up searching the premises for the reported lost children.

Just down the road is the George and Dragon pub, one of the most comfortable pubs in Shropshire, which deservedly does a roaring trade in lunches and evening meals. The ghost, however, belongs to a harsher time. Some years ago, opinions differ as to quite how many but it may have been in the 1880s, Much Wenlock was suffering a bit of a crime wave. Burglaries and break-ins were becoming alarmingly numerous, while travellers on the highway were increasingly likely to be held up at gunpoint.

The George and Dragon pub has stood in Much Wenlock's high street for longer than anyone can recall.

Obviously a gang of crooks had descended on the area and were dangerously active. Equally obviously, the good folk of Much Wenlock had to do something about it. They sent for the police, of course, but also took steps to protect themselves and their property. Some invested in guns, others in cudgels, while the landlord of the George and Dragon invested in a huge black dog of savage temperament.

To make doubly certain that his pub and his profits would be safe, the landlord kept the hound chained to an iron ring in the cellar during opening hours, tossing it only the merest scraps of food. Then he released it to roam the ground floor of the pub at night, content the dog would attack anyone who entered. Unknown to the landlord, however, his kitchen maid had taken pity on the dog. When nobody was watching, she would pop down to the cellar to feed offcuts and the occasional juicy steak to the poor, chained animal. It was the only love or attention the dog had in its life.

After the dog died, its ghost returned to the pub. It could be heard moving about in the cellar, the soft pad of its feet on stone followed by the gentle chinking of the chain it dragged around. Sometimes the phantom hound would emerge from the cellar to roam the pub, apparently in search of the young maid who had shown it some tenderness. As the years have passed it has been seen less often.

There are still times, however, when a great black dog will pad around the bar. Perhaps it may be mistaken for a dog belonging to one of the good country folk who make up the clientele, but those who know will recognise the phantom for what it is.

BARROW

The little hamlet of Barrow lies on the hills south-east of Much Wenlock among some of Shropshire's most attractive rolling countryside. This was for a long time some of the best hunting country in England, stocked with plenty of foxes and offering exciting, challenging riding for the huntsmen.

And nobody was a keener huntsman or a finer rider than local lad Tom Moody. Moody was a farm boy who, from an early age, showed a particular affinity with horses. He could calm the most spirited stallion with a word, or diagnose an ailment with a glance. Most impressive of all was his riding ability, getting the very best out of any horse he mounted and staying firmly in the saddle no matter what happened. He was plucked from his farm at Barrow by Squire George Forester of Willey, who saw young Tom riding across the fields one day.

Squire Forester gave the lad a job in his stables, then quickly transferred him to the hunt

The grave of Tom Moody at Barrow. This famous horseman is said to materialise beside the grave, then mount a spirited horse and ride off over the countryside he loved so much when alive.

where he became a legendary whipper-in. Moody was able to find a fox when nobody else could, and had only to twitch his whip to send the hounds off in pursuit. Indeed, the dogs obeyed his every command. Once Moody tumbled his horse into an old mine shaft. He was badly wounded and trapped, and nobody knew where he was. But the pack of hounds sensed something was wrong. Abandoning the scent of the fox, they tracked down Moody and ensured his rescue. Squire Forester basked in the admiration of his wealthy friends who enjoyed the sport to be had around Willey. Tom Moody enjoyed the hunt, and the coins that jingled into his hands as tips from satisfied visitors.

Tom Moody had a good life and a merry one, but all things must come to an end and in November 1796 Tom Moody lay dying. As his friends gathered round the deathbed, Moody asked for only one thing. 'When I am laid in my grave, let three halloos and horn blasts be given over me. For if Tom Moody does not lift his head, then Tom Moody is dead.'

On the day of the funeral the hunt turned out in all its finery, as did every hunting lady and gentleman who could get to Barrow churchyard in time. It was a magnificent funeral; with hundreds of horsemen, both gentry and yeomen forming a procession behind the coffin as it was carried up the hill to the church. As requested, the three halloos and horns were sounded. There was no movement from the grave, so the funeral service was concluded. Tom Moody lay in his grave and his admirers went home.

It did not last long. On crisp winter days when the local hunt is out and the sound of the hunting horn drifts over the Shropshire countryside, Tom Moody has been seen to appear quite suddenly beside his grave. He looks around as if seeking the source of the horn blasts, and then strides to the mounting block that stands beside the church gates. Climbing on to a great bay horse that materialises just in time, Moody trots off with a single foxhound following behind.

With foxhunting banned by Parliament in 2005, it remains to be seen if the restless spirit of Tom Moody will continue to rise.

IRONBRIDGE

The small town of Ironbridge is famous, of course, for its eponymous iron bridge. Erected in 1778 by Abraham Derby III, this was the world's first ever bridge made from iron. The fact that it still stands as firm and strong as when it was erected is a tribute to the skill of Shropshire's early ironworkers. It crosses the Severn where the river flows through a narrow limestone gorge of scenic beauty and has become one of the county's best-known landmarks.

The ghosts that move about here, however, are a grim bunch. And some of them predate the iron bridge by a good few years. The most horrific of the hauntings comes in the form of a boat drifting slowly

The eponymous iron bridge beneath which steers a macabre ghost boat.

down the Severn. Those who have seen it say that at first there seems little unusual about the craft. It is a large open boat, shaped rather like any other rowing boat apart from its size. Only as the craft comes closer, and many of those who see it peer down from the bridge, does it become clear that the boat is piled high with human corpses. Almost as soon as the grisly cargo is seen for what it is the boat seems to shiver, then fade rapidly from view.

It is thought that the phantom boat and is grim contents date to the last outbreak of plague that hit Shropshire in the 1660s. Thousands died in the outbreak, their bodies being taken downstream to vast 'plague pits' where they could be disposed of hygienically in an attempt to halt the spread of this dreaded disease.

The plague was a terrible disease that came and went in waves between its first arrival as the Black Death in the 1340s to the 1660s. It is generally thought to have been a variety of the bubonic plague that still occurs

The Tontine Hotel in Ironbridge, where a dramatic arrest led to a haunting.

infrequently in Asia in a mild form. It is now believed the plague is spread by rat fleas.

The symptoms were horrific. The first sign that something was wrong might have been a slight chill or fever. Within a day this would be followed by nausea and vomiting accompanied by a severe headache. The fever then returned with great intensity and some patients became delirious, running about screaming or writhing in agony. By the following day the tongue was coated in a white fur and a rash like dozens of red blisters covered the skin. About 48 hours later the buboes appeared. These were pus-filled growths that erupted in the armpits and groin. As they grew they became black and intensely painful to the touch. At this point the crisis was reached. If the buboes burst, which induced severe agony and burning pain, the patient stood a 50:50 chance of recovering. If, on the other hand, a series of bluish spots began to spread across the body, death was certain.

Records are incomplete, but it seems that in the space of 18 months Shropshire lost about 15 per cent of its population to plague. No wonder the voyages of the dreaded plague boats are recalled in spectral form on the River Severn, though why only at Ironbridge is unclear.

On the north bank of the river, facing out across the bridge, stands the elegant Tontine Hotel. This solid Georgian building, which has been there almost since the bridge was built, dominates the area and is a most comfortable place to stop and rest. One guest who halted here and stayed in Room 5 in the early Victorian period came to have reason to regret his stay. The man was wanted for a murder in Ketley and lodged here as he fled south towards Bristol to take ship abroad.

He had only got as far as the Tontine when the forces of law and order caught up with him. The burly policemen forced their way into his room, overpowered the murderer and dragged him off to face trial and execution at Shrewsbury. To this day there is said to be something odd about the room. Lights are switched on, and off, without help from human hands and strange noises may be heard. One guest awoke with the clear feeling that there was somebody else in the room, though there wasn't.

Just upstream of the Tontine is an old warehouse, now used as a centre for shops and light industry. The lane beside it runs down to the river, where boats were loaded and unloaded. It was formerly the custom for wagons parked here to be held in place by stout wooden chocks so that they did not inadvertently roll down into the river. Young boys were employed to hammer the chocks into place, or pull them free when no longer needed. One tragic day a wagon broke loose and crushed one of these boys to death. The plaintive spirit of the ragged boy is still to be seen trotting up and down the lane or along the riverbank.

Facing the Tontine across the bridge is the old cottage built to house the toll keeper who collected the pennies from those using the bridge. Today it houses the local tourist information office. There have been reports of a genteel lady in Victorian dress who pokes her head in here from time to time, accompanied by the distinct scent of lavender. She rarely stays long and does not call often, but is said to be a charming guest.

JACKFIELD

The village of Jackfield lies a couple of miles downstream of Ironbridge on the south bank of the Severn. Today it is best known for its impressive tile museum and associated shop, but two centuries ago it was an industrial centre every bit as important as Ironbridge or as Coalbrookdale on the north bank.

It was in these prosperous times that Lady Blythe, a local gentlewoman, decided that the factory workers deserved a splendid church in which to worship. She chose a site on top of the hill, appointed the architect and donated the money, but died before work could begin. After her death, the local parish council decided that it would be more convenient, if less spectacular, to site the church beside the river and alongside the factories rather than up on the hilltop.

Work began, supervised by the prominent Victorian architect Sir Arthur William Blomfield, who also built Portsmouth Cathedral. He chose to work in the French gothic style and made extensive use of the local bricks and tiles, available in a wide variety of colours to produce some strikingly ornamental designs.

Unfortunately, Lady Blythe did not take kindly to the revised site for the church. Her phantom was seen among the building works more than once and several workmen complained of

The church at Jackfield was constructed using the multi-coloured local bricks and tiles, but its founder was unhappy with the result and returns in spectral form to show her disappointment.

The spectres of two Victorian children play along Ferry Road at Jackfield.

The Boat Inn proudly boasts that time has little meaning here. It certainly has done nothing to put off the ghost that lurks within.

tools that went missing, or turned up in the most bizarre places. Nevertheless, the parish council insisted work continue on the new site and the church stands beside the river to this day. So does the ghost. Dressed in a long blue dress and wearing a bonnet the ghostly Lady Blythe stands to survey the church built with her money. Whether or not she approves of the final creation is unclear.

A few yards from the church, Ferry Road sweeps down to an old quay which formerly served a ferry across the river, but is now the site for a modern bridge. The haunting here recalls a tragedy that struck Jackfield in the 1840s. Two twins who lived in one of the cottages of Ferry Road were playing some game or other on

The blocked side door at the Boat Inn records the height of past floods that washed through Jackfield.

the heap of rejected tiles that lay piled up beside the factory. Suddenly the heap gave way, collapsing into the river and carrying the two children with it. Their drowned bodies were found next day caught in rushes on the riverbank just in front of their home cottage. They were holding hands.

It is the ghosts of these two children, which play and frolic along Ferry Road. Only their rather ragged and old-fashioned clothes pick them out as being anything other than a pair of jovial local children out for a lark.

The Boat Inn stands by the old ferry quay and boasts its own ghost. It is said that the Devil once stayed here in the guise of a wealthy gentleman, tempting locals to gamble with him. No doubt he was planning to trick them into gambling away their souls, but he was recognised in time and vanished. Whether the ghostly barmaid has anything to do with this infernal visitor is unclear. She seems pleasant enough as she moves around the downstairs area. Very often she beckons a witness forward. One woman who saw the ghost was rather braver than the rest and followed the spectre. When she reached the ghost, however, it simply vanished without imparting any message at all.

BADGER

T he church at Badger stands beside a wide pond, fringed by rushes and inhabited by ducks and geese. Beyond the pond once stood the elegant Georgian mansion of Badger Hall. The old house is gone

The church at Badger occupies one of the most charming sites of any church in Shropshire.

now, having been demolished in the 1930s, but its site and the route to the church are still haunted by the beautiful Grey Lady of Badger.

When she is seen, the ghost is so lifelike that some have mistaken her for a real person. She has long, golden hair that falls in waves to her back and has a charming smile that some believe has a somewhat sad tinge to it. Her dress is long and full in the skirt, though tighter around the body. Although widely known as the Grey Lady of Badger, her dress is often said to be cream or even pale pink in colour.

The grey lady of Badger wears a full skirt that may date her to the 18th century.

It is not entirely clear who this lady was, nor why she flits so restlessly between the old manor and the lake-side church. However, when the hall was being demolished workmen found a stout wooden casket hidden beneath some flagstones. Inside was hidden an impressively large engagement ring. Did this hark back to some broken engagement that led to a broken heart? We don't know, but given the sad smile of the beautiful young lady ghost of Badger, it is more than likely.

BECKBURY

Beckbury lies in the valley of the River Worfe on the far eastern edge of Shropshire. It is one of those villages that is on the way to nowhere in particular and so is found only by those who are going there.

The road running through Beckbury is haunted by a colourful former squire of the village.

For many years, until 1896, the manor and estates here were in the hands of the Stubbs family. It was Squire Walter Stubbs, born here in 1671, who was to be the most noteworthy of the family. His generosity, sense of humour and extrovert character combined to make him as well known as he was well liked and admired.

For some reason the phantom horseman who rides through the village, past the ancient church and on to Lower Hall is always said to be Squire Stubbs. The identification is odd, as the horseman is never seen, only heard. The sounds of passing hoof beats, jingling harness and a spirited whinnying are heard often enough, but as the rider is not seen it is difficult to know how he can be identified. However, some ghosts are known to fade with age.

Perhaps Squire Stubbs once appeared in all his finery so that locals were able to recognise him, but now only the sounds of his passing are heard.

HOPTON CASTLE

The English Civil War of the 1640s was a nasty affair. Thousands of men died in battle, many more from disease, and all too many troops were given to plundering innocent civilians if they got the chance. It was not, however, a genocidal slaughter. The officers and men of the time knew the rules of war and, more often than not, abided by them.

Which makes what happened at Hopton Castle all the more shocking. It is no wonder that it led to a haunting.

The castle was already 500 years old when its owners, the staunchly puritanical Wallop family, declared for Parliament and welcomed Colonel Samuel Moore and 30 Roundhead troopers. In the spring of 1644 a force of 500 royalists descended on Hopton Castle under Sir Michael Woodhouse and a Mr Sutton, about whom little is known other than his name. The royalists held York, Newcastle and Liverpool in the north as well as much of southern England, but their lines of communication between the two were continually threatened by Roundhead forces in the midlands. Woodhouse had firm instructions from King Charles himself: Hopton Castle must be taken, and taken quickly.

It was not to be. Moore had not wasted his time. He had updated the ancient defences with earthen ramparts, deep trenches and carefully-sited guns. The royalists made little headway, even when they tried tunnelling under the defences. Time dragged by. Woodhouse was losing his patience, and any chance he had of impressing the king and getting some suitable reward.

Finally, after almost a month of siege, Moore asked for a parley. His food was running out and starvation was only days away. Rather than put his men through such suffering merely to delay surrender, Moore offered to surrender Hopton Castle promptly on the condition that he and his men were allowed to march out with their honour intact and were given 24 hours head start before a pursuit began. It was a not unusual deal in the warfare of the times and several other fortresses in England had already changed hands under similar terms. Eager to get hold of Hopton Castle and move on, Woodhouse and Sutton agreed.

Moore opened the gates and marched out at the head of his men. It was with considerable shock that the Parliamentarians found themselves faced by the levelled guns of the royalists. Protesting loudly, Moore was tied hand and foot, then thrown over a horse and hauled off to Ludlow Castle to be cast into prison. His men were likewise tied up, then had their throats slit and were tossed into a nearby pond. One man survived this barbaric treatment, a Major Phillips, while a wounded soldier who had chosen to stay in Hopton Castle quickly hid until the royalists had gone.

The Roundhead soldiers of Hopton Castle perished in one of the most notorious atrocities of the English Civil War.

A maid who had been working in the castle was forced to watch the brutal treatment of the defenders, then was tied up and dragged along behind Woodhouse's horse. She had been spared only to repeat the horrific tale to the garrison of the next castle on Woodhouse's list, Brampton Castle in Herefordshire.

Before he left, Woodhouse set fire to the castle and ordered his engineers to blast a hole in the defences with gunpowder. He left it as the ruin it is today.

He also left the ghosts. Most of these are, unsurprisingly, of the men betrayed and murdered. Walking with bowed heads, the little column of men has been seen to march out of the castle gates, turn to the left and then fade away. Presumably they vanish where they died so long ago.

A few people claim to have seen a ghost down by the pond where the bodies were hidden. This is generally thought to be the phantom of a young woman named Elizabeth Mayrick. She was engaged to be married to one of the Parliamentarian soldiers killed at Hopton Castle. When news of the atrocity spread, young Miss Mayrick hurried to the village to see if she could find any trace of her beloved. The villagers pointed out the pond, and she is said to have spent days weeping bitter tears beside the still waters before dying of a broken heart.

The tragic story has a rather satisfactory ending. Prince Rupert, the king's commander in the west, was appalled by the murders. He promptly had Woodhouse and Sutton stripped of their commands, but sadly failed to put them on trial. Destiny was calling Prince Rupert north to Marston Moor and a defeat that spelled the end of the king's hopes of victory in the war.

BROMFIELD

The ghost of Bromfield is one of those enigmatic phantoms about which more is known than seen. She is mentioned in several books on ghosts in Shropshire, and has found her way on to at least one radio show, but finding details about the lady in Bromfield itself is not easy.

The phantom is said to be that of a Mrs Holland who died in one of the charming little cottages of the village in the early years of the 20th century. She was, it would appear, an inoffensive soul who quietly pottered about the village maintaining as genteel an air as her fading wealth would support.

She is thought to have habitually worn widow's garb for the last few years of her life in honour of her husband. After her death the figure of an elderly lady in black was seen walking slowly along the lanes. This was the ghost of Mrs Holland. She seems to have been seen quite regularly for a few years, but there are no recent reports of her being particularly active.

LUDLOW

Without doubt Ludlow is one of the most charming towns in Shropshire, indeed in England. It stands perched on top of a hill almost surrounded by the waters of the Teme and Corve rivers. Over 1000 years ago this hilltop was fortified against raiding Welshmen, but it was in 1085 that Roger Montgomery, Earl of Shrewsbury, began to build the mighty castle that dominates the town to this day.

It is appropriate that the ghosts of Ludlow begin at the castle, though the custodians prefer not to talk about them to any great extent. The best-known haunting dates back to the reign of King Henry II in the 12th century. King Henry was often in France administering his vast lands in that country, and the Welsh would take advantage of his absence to raid into England. At other times, peace returned and the Welsh were welcome visitors to Ludlow market.

It was in more peaceful times that a Welsh knight met and fell in love with Marion de la Bruyère, a wealthy Norman damsel living in Ludlow Castle. The girl returned his affections and soon a love affair was in full swing. Then troubled times returned and the Welsh were banned from entering within the town walls of Ludlow. Nothing daunted, young Marion let down a rope over the battlements of the castle so that her lover could visit her still.

For a time, all went well. But one night the Welshman arrived with his sword and a gang of armed men. Clearly, they were intent on capturing the castle and opening the route into England for a Welsh raid of significant scope. Realising she had been betrayed by the man she loved, Marion drew his sword and stabbed him through the chest. She then raised the alarm before throwing herself to her death from the battlements.

73

The poor, distraught ghost of Marion de la Bruyère is said to haunt the castle, as well she might. The ghostly manifestations most often reported are the sounds of a woman gasping for breath, perhaps in a fight or struggle, and Marion herself is seen only rarely.

The ghost of Marion de la Bruyère is seen more often in the churchyard of St Laurence, one of the county's largest and most magnificent medieval churches. She is not alone. The phantom of an elderly lady wearing what would appear to be a blue dressing gown also frequents the area, shuffling among the tombs.

Nearby, in Corve Street, stands St Leonard's Chapel. This small building has been deconsecrated and put to secular use, but this has done nothing to deter the phantom that haunts the area.

The walls of Ludlow were proof against any attack but not the treachery that led to the haunting at the castle.

This is the ghost of William Owen, a hugely successful portrait painter who became the favourite of King George IV in his days as Prince Regent. Owen was born in Ludlow and returned there whenever his work permitted.

It was on one such visit that Owen fell ill with a minor sickness. The local doctor prescribed a medicine to cure the painter and sent a boy off to the chemist that was then in Corve Street to fetch it. Tragically, the boy picked up the wrong bottle and inadvertently gave Owen deadly poison instead of medicine. Realising something was wrong, Owen set out for the

The gateway to a small chapel, haunted by the phantom of a dying man whose last wish was to reach this holy place.

chemist's shop, but the poison overpowered him before he got there. He turned in towards the chapel, perhaps seeking divine aid, and fell dead.

It is Owen whose ghost has been seen hurrying along the pavement as if in urgent need, then turning aside towards the chapel. He is, it must be assumed, recreating his last fatal journey.

Some years before Owen's accident, another man came to Ludlow only to pass away. Nobody can now recall his name, but he was a gentleman of wealth and property who commanded troops in the army of King Charles I during the Civil War. He was captured at some battle or other and brought to Ludlow Castle for safekeeping. As was common in those days, the gentleman gave his word he would not leave the town and so was released from his cell. He took up lodgings at the Globe Inn where his money bought him fine food and wines to compensate him for his lengthy imprisonment. After some months, the gentleman fell ill and died.

His ghost, complete with lace shirt and velvet jacket walks the ground floor as if in search of a good meal. Given the Globe's welcoming character and fine menu it is hardly surprising the old boy has never left. A second ghost is said to lurk upstairs, wandering the corridors at night with a lit candle in his hand. Whether this is the same man or some other phantom is not clear.

Equally obscure is the identity of the ghost at the Bull Inn. The haunting seems to be linked to the discovery of a priest's hole in the 1960s. These priests' holes were tiny chambers secreted under floors or within walls and were just large enough to hide a man. Traditionally they are said to have hidden Catholic priests, hence their name, during the days when the religious wars of the 16th and 17th centuries encouraged some Catholics to seek the assassination of England's Protestant kings and nobles. In fact, many 'priests' holes' were for hiding highwaymen, smuggled goods and other contraband.

The Globe Inn at Ludlow is home to an exceptionally well-dressed spectre.

The history of the priest's hole at the Bull Inn is unknown, but given the date of the fireplace where it was found it would seem to be 17th century in date. Soon after it was found in the course of rebuilding work, disembodied footsteps began to be heard about the building and at least one person reported being tapped on the arm by an invisible companion.

KNOWBURY

The phantom schoolgirl of Knowbury is seen most often around the school, but never in it, which must have been a relief for teachers struggling to keep order in a class.

She is said to be aged about 11 years old and to wear a white pinafore dress with full sleeves and, according to some, lacy cuffs and collar. In other words, a fairly typical country girl of the later Victorian era. This ghost was usually seen walking slowly or standing quietly at various spots near the school and St Paul's church. In the 1950s an outbreak of poltergeist activity in a house in the village was blamed on the girl, though why was never entirely clear.

Visible phantoms do not tend to throw objects around very often, or to indulge in the many other tricks of the typical poltergeist. In any case the nuisance soon faded, though the ghost remains. Even the closure of the village school has not persuaded this ancient pupil to depart.

KINLET

The man known as 'The Terror of Scotland' came from the village of Kinlet in the shape of Sir George Blount, gentleman. This imposing man earned his name during the so-called 'rough wooing' of the 1540s.

King Henry VIII of England wanted his son and heir to marry the infant Mary, Queen of Scots, and so unite the two nations. The Scots, however, preferred a French alliance and refused. King Henry sent the English army into Scotland to take the bride by force. The invasion culminated in the Battle of Pinkie, just outside Edinburgh, after Henry's death when his army was led by the Earl of Somerset. The English destroyed the Scots army, killing some 10,000 men while losing only 247 themselves.

Then troops of men, one led by Sir George Blount of Kinlet, fanned out across the kingdom to find the intended bride. Mary had, however, already fled to France, but that did not stop the English taking possession of the northern lands. Blount administered the areas assigned to him with a ruthless efficiency that gained him his nickname. In 1561 Queen Mary returned to Scotland, having reached an agreement with the new ruler of England, Queen Elizabeth I.

The church of Kinlet lies more than a mile outside the village. It is here that Sir George Blount is buried and where his ghost begins its oft-repeated journey.

Blount, in his turn, returned home to Kinlet. There he married and settled down to farm his spreading estates. The marriage produced a son and daughter. The boy died as a toddler, tragically choking on an apple. Despite his fearsome reputation, Blount was distraught. He laid the tiny body in a silver coffin and buried it with his own hands. When his daughter grew up, Blount was pained to see her form an attachment with a local man of whom he disapproved.

As Blount lay dying in 1581 he called his daughter to his side and begged her not to marry the man. His pleas fell on deaf ears. Barely was he cold in his grave at Kinlet Church when his daughter married. It was this event that began the hauntings.

Emerging from the church in an apparent furious temper, the ghostly Sir George Blount calls to his side a huge black charger. Mounting the steed, Sir George puts his spurs to the horse and gallops off at high speed towards the

The long, winding road that runs from Kinlet Church to the village. It is along this road that the dramatic phantom has been seen riding.

village of Kinlet. The first time the ghost put in an appearance, it nearly frightened to death the old family servant who saw it. The dramatic ghost continued to ride long after the errant daughter passed away and, in 1720, the Blounts pulled down the old house in an attempt to escape the ghostly visitations.

Mary, Queen of Scots. It was while searching for this queen that the squire of Kinlet earned his nickname 'Terror of Scotland'.

The new Kinlet Hall is an imposing structure in the finest neoclassical taste. But its construction has done nothing to halt the appearances of Sir George Blount. Mounted on his fiery steed, he rides the road between the church and hall to this day. It is as well not to get in his way, for he is said to charge down any who do, hurling them aside with terrific force. Clearly the old warrior's anger is not yet faded.

ALVELEY

The village of Alveley lies strung out along the old main road south of Bridgnorth, where the hills crowd down to the flood plain of the River Severn. It is on Astley Bank, one of the lanes that run down the hills, that the most dramatic of the Alveley ghosts is to be seen.

This ghost is of a tall man dressed all in black and wearing a wide-brimmed hat, also black. He strides along with great purpose, as if determined to get somewhere with some urgency. Where he is going and why are as enigmatic as his identity. This is simply one of those ghosts which stalk out of the supernatural world whence they come, march across the mortal world, then fade again a few seconds later.

More easily identifiable is the phantom horseman who rides up the lane from Alveley towards Coton Hall to the east. Riding a prancing white pony of apparent good temper, this young teenage lad wears a suit of 19th-century cut. This is the ghost of a boy who lived at Coton Hall in Victorian times and was given a white pony for Christmas one year. Just a few days later, the pony was found wandering riderless along the lane. A search soon found the body of the boy lying in the roadway near the foot of the hill beneath a tree. Quite what happened was never discovered, but the boy's neck was broken and his forehead had suffered a heavy blow.

It was put down as just another riding accident, until the ghost began to appear. Local gossip soon had it that there had been foul play of some kind

A youthful horseman rides up the hill towards the gates of Coton Hall.

involved in the boy's death, and that this had led to the haunting. If so, the ghost does not communicate in any obvious fashion, by pointing at a place or speaking for instance. He simply rides up the lane as if without a care in the world.

BRIDGNORTH

As with so many towns in Shropshire, Bridgnorth was built on a hilltop for protection against marauding Welsh armies. And like many others it has a castle dating to Norman times, though in the case of Bridgnorth only shattered ruins remain as a result of a visit paid by Cromwellian troops during the Civil War of the 1640s.

The ghosts are nowhere near as old as either town or castle. The oldest are also the youngest. The phantoms of two young children date back to a

Now a shop, Abanazer's Cottage is haunted by the man who built it.

flood in the 1650s. Trapped in a room from which they could not escape, the poor children were drowned. Since then, however, their phantoms have been seen playing happily in Cartway, the steep street where the tragedy happened. Their life on earth may have ended, but they seem to continue their games and high spirits in spectral form throughout the ages.

Just as welcoming is the ghost to be found at the 200-year-old Abanazer's Cottage, now a florist's, near the foot of Cartway. This spectre is generally thought to be that of the eponymous Abanazer, who had the house built at the foot of the precipice on which the castle is perched in the reign of King George III. The ghost usually keeps himself to the attic and makes no more disturbance than a few footsteps in the dead of night. Just occasionally, however, the ghost comes down the stairs to wander the first floor and the shop.

Old Abanazer comes as an inoffensive old man dressed in a dark suit and breeches. He bustles up or down the stairs as if on some business of his own. Perhaps he loves the house that he built so much that he does not wish to leave.

Altogether more sinister is the ghost at the Crown and Raven public house. It is not that she causes any trouble, far from it. The pub is a welcoming and charming building that offers fine fare to any who care to drop by. But she has a tragic and sombre history.

The ghost goes by the name of Evie and appears as a rather pretty young woman who walks through the bar in something of a hurry, and will sometimes call out as if trying to attract somebody's attention. This is the ghost of a servant employed here some 150 years ago who had the misfortune to catch her

Croft Hotel in Bridgnorth is haunted by spectral horses recalling when this site was put to a very different use.

fiancé kissing another girl. In a fit of jealous rage Evie stabbed her rival, and then her fiancé. The man survived, but the girl died. Evie was duly tried for murder and hanged by a stern justice system.

It seems that she returns to haunt the place where she worked so happily before tragedy overtook her.

Close off the high street is St Mary's Street in which stands a fine old building that is now the Croft Hotel. In years gone by, this was the old fire station for Bridgnorth. What are now cottages and rooms to let were then the stables for the horses that pulled the fire engine. The station was abandoned when motorised transport took over the emergency role, but the ghostly horses remain. Even today there will sometimes come the sound of a loud bell, followed by stamping hooves and excited whinnying of horses getting ready for sudden action. Nothing is ever seen, but the noises are real enough.

ASTLEY ABBOTS

Some strange tragedy led to the double haunting at Astley Abbots, though exactly what happened has never been discovered. The events began innocently enough on a summer's Sunday in early Victorian days. The vicar stopped a young couple who were due to be married in three weeks' time and suggested that they might like to come to the church one evening to discuss the service and anything that they might require in the way of organ music or bells.

The girl, Hannah Phillips, lived just beyond the Severn near Lower Allscot. Come the agreed evening, she set off from home to cross the shallow ford and walk up to the church. At Astley Abbots her fiancé and the vicar awaited her arrival. To please his bride-to-be, the fiancé was dressed in his new wedding suit. The two men waited, and waited, but young Hannah did not arrive.

As the long summer evening began to turn to dusk, the worried men set out along the path Hannah should be taking from her home to the church. They found nothing. No sign of Hannah or any indication that anything might have happened to her. The girl was never seen again. It was supposed that she must have slipped when crossing the Severn and drowned in the deep waters below the ford, but nobody ever really knew.

Over the years since, the ghost of poor Hannah Phillips has been seen frequently following the fatal path from her home, over the Severn and on to the church. It is perhaps odd that the ghost should walk all the way to the church when, in reality, Hannah never got there. Perhaps the spectre is tracing the steps that the girl was determined to cover, rather than the route she actually did take. Or perhaps Hannah Phillips was not drowned in the Severn but came to a grim death nearer the church.

The lane leading up to the church at Astley Abbots is haunted by a young woman with a tragic story.

Be that as it may, it is known that her fiancé died soon after the tragedy. His ghost appears too, hovering beside the road near the church. Presumably he is waiting for his beloved Hannah, just as he waited for so many fruitless hours all those years ago.

MORVILLE

There is no mistaking the Acton Arms public house. It stands boldly beside the A458 where that road swoops down into a valley to pass through Morville on its way south to Bridgnorth. And fixed solidly to the front wall of the pub is a large wooden panel bearing the painted arms in question.

Quite who the ghost at this pub might be is unclear, but he is certainly very active. He is an elderly man who likes to sit around in the bar, which can come as no surprise given its warm welcome and fine selection of ales and meals. He is seen several times each year, though sometimes merely as a silhouette or shadow.

One of the clearest sightings came in 2002. A teenage daughter of the landlord had the job of giving the bar a good clean through before it opened in the morning. On Saturday she was cleaning in the bar when she heard humming. She thought her father had got up early and did not really pay much attention to it, so she heard it for a good few minutes before she moved around the corner of the room to come in view of the bar. Seated on a stool with his back to the bar and looking out of the window was an old man, who was humming a tune. The girl was scared and fled the room while the old man continued to hum and ignore her completely. She later recalled that the old man was quite distinct and real, but seemed to be without substance. 'He was watery-looking, like seeing somebody through the bottom of a glass.'

Others have seen this gentle old man, and some small objects have been moved around the bar without being touched by human hands. On one occasion the barman was sweeping the floor after closing time. He had got the litter and dust into a tidy pile and set off in search of the dustpan. It was not in its usual cupboard, so the barman returned to the bar only to find the dustpan on the floor with the litter neatly swept into it.

In the private upstairs area, there seem to be two other ghosts. These ghosts are heard, but rarely seen. The more frequently heard is a very well-spoken lady who chatters away as if talking to somebody. Only very rarely can her words be caught clearly, and then they seem to be fairly routine domestic chatter. On one occasion the landlady of the pub was in her bedroom when she heard very clearly a child running along the corridor outside, although she knew she was alone in the building at the time. The footsteps were followed by a sudden crash and a squeal of pain. 'Mummy, I've hurt my arm,' said a little girl's voice. 'Oh dear. Now we shall be late,' replied the voice of the well-spoken lady.

Then absolute silence descended over the Acton Arms. A quick investigation proved that the landlady was, as she had thought, quite alone in the pub. A former landlord reported that he once saw this phantom lady

The calm exterior of the Acton Arms belies the supernatural activity within.

coming up the stairs. She was wearing a long black skirt with short, lace up boots and seemed to be of Victorian date.

Elsewhere in the village is to be found the shade of Prior Richard Manners, or it might be that of Sir Richard Manners. Or, just possibly, the two men are one and the same, it is difficult to tell. Prior Richard Manners was the last prior of Morville Priory, a relatively small but well run religious house in the 16th century. As with all the other monasteries in England, Morville Priory was closed down by King Henry VIII in the course of his dispute with the Pope that led to England becoming a Protestant nation. Prior Manners was, by all accounts, diligent at his work and ran the monastic estates efficiently and profitably.

Sir Richard Manners, on the other hand, was the 4th son of the 12th Lord Ros and brother of the 1st Earl of Rutland. He, too, was efficient and hard working. But he was a devout Protestant who bought up a number of monastic properties from King Henry VIII. He converted them into a highly profitable inheritance that he passed on to his children. Among these properties was the old Morville Priory, so recently vacated by Prior Richard Manners.

It is possible, some might say likely, that the prior and the knight were one and the same. That having divested himself of his religious office, the young man got married and bought up his former home. The records are incomplete, so we shall probably never be certain. But there can be no doubt that one of the Richard Manners of Morville returns in spectral form to walk from the village to the parish church, a distance to the west over low lying fields.

EASTHOPE

I
f you are thinking of moving to the charming little village of Easthope, you had best be prepared for a spectral visitor. Several people who have decided to come to live in this village perched on the slopes of Wenlock Edge have found themselves approached by the village ghost, who comes just once as if to inspect them and see if they are good enough to live in his old parish.

The monks' graves at Easthope, where fighting phantoms can startle passers-by.

This ghost is of William Germston, who was the vicar here in the 14th century. He did not get on very well with the lord of the manor, one Sir John de Easthope. The two men clashed repeatedly over land rights, rents due and the treatment of the local peasants. One night in 1333 the two men became locked in a particularly violent quarrel, which ended with Sir John striking William such a blow that the man fell down dead. Overcome by remorse at what he had done, Sir John committed suicide a few days later.

It is the ghost of the victim who returns to walk the churchyard and lanes of this village. He appears in a long robe, which reaches to the ground, and walks around with a fairly determined stride. He is described as being quite short and with cropped, dark hair.

As a good vicar, he likes to keep an eye on his parish. It may be for this reason that he is seen most often by newcomers. One recently-arrived resident was startled to see the phantom clergyman walk into his house, and then vanish into thin air. Thankfully William Germston's appearances are not usually so alarming.

The other phantoms of Easthope are rather more violent. These two burly men are seen locked in combat among the tombs of the churchyard. They wrestle, punch and kick with abandoned ferocity as if determined to inflict serious injury on each other. This is exactly what they did back in the 15th century.

The two men were monks from Much Wenlock Abbey who came to Easthope to supervise the collection of rents from the abbey's lands in the village. As was usual for the visiting monks, they stayed at the local hostelry. As was far from usual, these two monks indulged in heavy drinking, and then began gambling. An argument broke out and the fight began. In the course of the struggle, the monks fell down the stone steps to the cellar and both were killed. The fatal struggle is now recreated in spectral form beside the graves of the two monks, marked by two stone slabs that carry no inscription other than a simple cross inside a circle.

WILDERHOPE

The beautiful old manor of Wilderhope stands tucked under the steep slopes of Wenlock Edge, the great ridge that runs for miles across southern Shropshire. The magnificent old building is now a youth hostel, but in years gone by was one of the grander houses of the local gentry.

In 1647 it was home to one Major Smallman, lately of the army of His Majesty King Charles I. The Civil War in which Major Smallman had fought so gallantly was now over. The unfortunate, and so often foolish, King Charles was a prisoner of Parliament and would soon be put on trial, to be found guilty and beheaded in London. There were numerous plots to get the king free from prison and spirit him away over the sea to safety. Spies employed by Parliament fingered Major Smallman as being involved in one such plot.

When the Parliamentarian troopers came calling for Major Smallman, they put him under house arrest in his own manor. Fearing for both his liberty and his life, Smallman slipped away. Mounting a horse, he put his spurs to the steed and galloped off along Wenlock Edge. Unfortunately for the fugitive, a second Roundhead patrol was approaching and came across the Major just where the road runs along the very lip of the precipice. Smallman hauled back on his reins, the horse came to a slithering stop but lost its footing and plunged over the 100-ft cliff.

The Roundheads peered gingerly over the edge, to see the horse smashed to pulp on the rocks below. They did not see the gallant Major caught in the branches of a small crab apple tree projecting from the cliff. Thinking the man dead, Parliament's men abandoned the manor of Wilderhope and rode home.

Managing to escape his precarious perch with a struggle, Smallman crept home. After a few days in hiding to arrange his affairs, Smallman disguised himself and fled to the continent. Like so many other royalist gentlemen, Smallman spent the following years earning his living with his sword in foreign armies until King Charles II regained his father's throne and it was safe to come home at last to the beautiful Shropshire countryside.

The ghost that lurks on Wenlock Edge above Wilderhope Manor is not that of Major Smallman, but of his horse. The great black stallion gallops out of the manor, along the drive and on to the lane that leads to Much Wenlock. Racing at full speed the mighty spectral horse tears along with ears laid back and eyes staring wildly. Any who get in its way are well advised to step aside, for the phantom has the power to throw them aside with terrific force. Reaching the spot of the fatal fall, the horse turns off the road and hurls itself off the cliff into empty air. Which is where it abruptly vanishes.

A startling phantom indeed.

It is from Wilderhope Manor that the ghostly charger begins its journey up to the commanding heights of Wenlock Edge.

RATLINGHOPE

The little village of Ratlinghope hides away amid the wild country west of the Long Mynd. It is a small place, and always was. The tiny church of St Margaret's rarely had its own vicar and was usually served by the clergymen of Woolstaston or Church Stretton.

It is thought that this arrangement may have led to the haunting, though nobody is certain. The road leading north-east out of Ratlinghope climbs up the slopes of the Long Mynd before dividing so that the northern branch runs on to Woolstaston while the southern branch runs on over the heights to Church Stretton.

It is on this road that a funeral procession is sometimes seen. The hearse is pulled by horses and the mourners following in its wake are dressed in formal clothes of a Victorian date. The procession is usually seen only from a distance as it moves slowly up the hill, but once or twice has been seen at closer quarters.

Whose funeral this might be and why it returns in phantom form are quite mysterious.

STIPERSTONES

Standing high and windswept on the hills of south-western Shropshire are the Stiperstones. Geologists are certain these are a natural outcrop of very hard quartzite stone, but locals are certain they are supernatural in origin.

On the slopes of the hills is a deep, narrow gully known as Hell's Gutter. This contains an opening that, it is said, leads directly down to Hell itself and is one of the places where the Devil and his minions pour forth to do their evil on earth, and into which they drag the souls of those wicked folk who are doomed to spend eternity in the fires of hell.

The enigmatic Stiperstones around which so many legends swirl are, in fact, natural outcrops of tough quartzite rock.

One day, the Devil became exasperated by the fact that humans would gather at Hell's Gutter to keep a watch for him and his demons so that they could hide in churches to be safe from him. If he could hide the entrance to Hell, the Devil reasoned, he could slip in and out unnoticed. He gathered together a great pile of stones in Ireland and began carrying them over to Shropshire to block up Hell's Gutter. However, he soon grew tired of the work, and dumped the stones on the hills instead to form the Stiperstones.

On the longest night of the year, the ghosts, witches and demons of Shropshire come here to pay homage to their evil master. They gather in a great circle to discuss the events of the past year and to plan their evil for the coming twelve months. People out on the night of 21 December have seen lights moving around among the Stiperstones and the shadowy figures prancing about. It is wise to avoid the place at night, however, for the demons curse all those that they see, causing death within a year.

LINLEY

Nestled in a gentle fold of land west of the glowering heights of the Long Mynd, Linley is a surprisingly sheltered spot. It may be this that attracts the phantom lady dressed in white who walks the lanes in and around the village.

The ghost is seen with some regularity, walking slowly along her chosen path or road and ignoring any mere mortal who happens to be about. One witness said that she was dressed in a long dress of an off-white or cream colour. It was clearly made of a lightweight material for it flapped and shifted as the lady walked along. As the ghostly lady approached the witness, she suddenly seemed to move sideways, then vanished from sight.

On a few occasions the lady is accompanied by a great black dog, which pads along beside her. This is a frightful beast with long, shaggy hair and large eyes that seem to be human rather than animal.

The lady may appear gentle enough, but it is probably wise to avoid her. You never know when the hound may appear.

The long lane into Linley is the haunt of a gentle spectre.

• Index •